A Foreign Visitor's Survival Guide to America

SHAUNA SINGH BALDWIN

MARILYN M. LEVINE

John Muir Publications
Santa Fe, NM 87504

John Muir Publications, P.O. Box 613, Santa Fe, NM 87504

© 1992 by Shauna Singh Baldwin and Marilyn M. Levine
Cover © 1992 by John Muir Publications
All rights reserved.
Printed in the United States of America
First edition. First printing September 1992

Library of Congress Cataloging-in-Publication Data
Baldwin, Shauna Singh.
   A foreign visitor's survival guide to America / Shauna Singh
  Baldwin, Marilyn M. Levine. — 1st ed.
    p. cm.
   Includes bibliographical references and index.
   ISBN 1-56261-059-7
   1. Visitors, Foreign—United States—Life skills guides.
2. United States—Guidebooks.   I. Levine, Marilyn M.   II. Title.
E158.B29   1992
973.928—dc20   92-30032
                                                                                    CIP

Distributed to the book trade by
W. W. Norton & Co.
New York, New York

Design: Susan Gutnik
Typeface: Palatino
Typography: Copygraphics, Inc.
Illustrations: Richard Lange
Printer: McNaughton & Gunn, Inc.
Cover design: Ken Wilson
Cover photo: Leo de Wys, Inc./Steve Vidler

Contents

Preface vii

Acknowledgments ix

1 **Preparation and Arrival** 1
Packing and Dressing for Your Journey—Welcome to the U.S.A.—Dealing With Border Officials—First Impressions—Meeting Americans—Evaluating Sources of Information in America—A Few Details

2 **Dining Out** 14
Commercial Dining Places—Cafeterias—Meal Plans for College Students—Bars and Nightclubs—Dining at Someone's Home—Barbecues—Brunches—Some Minor Points

3 **Communicating** 23
The Telephone—The Post Office—Sending a Telegram

4 **Getting Around** 35
Maps and Transit Routes—Transportation

5 **Housing** 46
Hotels or Motels—Hostels—Dormitories and Residence Halls—Shared Accommodations—Apartment Hotels—Your Own Apartment—Furnishing Your New Home—Housing for Couples with Children—Disputes and Rights

6 **Cooking at Home** 60
Equipping Your Kitchen—Your Relationship with the Food Store—Disposing of Packaging—Appliances—Recipes—Cleaning Up

7 **Keeping Clean** 73
Personal Cleanliness—Doing Laundry—Dusting and Vacuuming—Cleaning for Sanitary Purposes—Creepy Crawlers

8 Clothing 83
Headcoverings—Hairstyles—Seasons and Temperatures—Fashion—Dressing for Different Occasions—Sales

9 Working in America 96
Foreign Students—Permanent Residents—The Job Search—Interviewing—Buying a Job—Technical Skills—On the Job in Corporate America

10 Buying a Vehicle 114
Getting a Car Loan—Basic Car Care—Car Safety—Car Theft—Accidents

11 Health and Medical Care 121
Routine Health Care and Fitness—Small Problems—Finding a Doctor—Diagnostic Tests—Clinics and Hospitals—Life-Threatening Emergencies—Paying for Medical Care—Dental Care—The Doctor-Patient Relationship—Living Wills

12 Managing Your Money 135
Financial Institutions—Money Orders and Check Cashing—Overseas Money Transfers—Opening an Account—Writing Checks—Keeping Records—Debit Cards and Automated Teller Machines—Credit Cards and Borrowing—Taxes—Buying ''On Time''—Gambling, Lotteries, Sweepstakes—Life Insurance—Wills—Charity

13 Social Customs and the Law 153
Men and Women—Marriage—Divorce—Birth—Death—Religion in American Life

14 Safety and Dealing with Emergencies 166
Getting Locked Out—Plumbing Problems—Electricity Failures—Home Burglaries—Fire—Medical Emergencies—Emergencies Requiring Police Assistance

15 Difficult Situations 174
Immigration Questioning and Arrests—Child Abuse and Neglect—Wife Battering and Sexual Assault—Drugs and Alcohol—Depression—Other Problems

16 Beyond Survival 180

Appendix 191
Information Sources—Minimum Kitchen Equipment List—A Food Shopping List for Survival—A Bathroom Shopping List—Dress Formality Categories—International Driver's Licenses—Voluntary Agencies in Major Cities—Important Dates in the United States—American Cooking Terms—Glossary—Clothing Sizes, U.S. and Metric—U.S. Customary Weight and Measures/Metric Conversions

Suggested Reading 204

Suggested Videotapes 205

Index 208

Preface

Why should you buy a book about living in the United States? Many newcomers have adjusted quite well without one—including one of the authors of this book. Learning to function in a new culture is a little like learning to ride a bicycle. It looks so easy when you see others riding one, but it is hard to believe you will be able to avoid the potholes and puddles or even go through them just for the fun of it. But wasn't learning to ride a bicycle easier when you had a friendly person or two to help? We are like that someone who taught you how to ride your bicycle. This book is our explanation of the principles of this culture and our shout of encouragement.

As a newcomer, if you knew what questions to ask, you would. And if your American friends or colleagues or teachers knew you did not know something, they would tell you. But since you do not know what it is that you do not know, and *they* do not know what you do not know, you do not know what questions to ask. And they do not tell you, since they do not know you do not know.

Foreign students and new immigrants will find this book useful since it is about accommodating your cultural differences rather than suppressing them. At every step, we discuss the reactions you are likely to have and suggest ways to adjust your expectations and avoid cultural misunderstandings. Armed with the information in this book, you will be in control of your own degree of adjustment and will be able to function easily.

A note about style: We have tried not to assume any particular country of origin for our readers, as America's newcomers are from all over the world. We use the terms "America" and "the U.S.A." interchangeably for ease of reference, with no offense intended to the other countries of North and South America. We have tried to include explanations or pronunciations within sentences for words that may require them. International English equivalents of American words are included in the text where possible.

In the chapters that follow, we will present both information and advice. Remember that ours is only one perspective and that you should not consider this book an authority on all the subjects we discuss simply because you see the advice in print. Ours is a point of view, influenced by our experiences in America, our cultures of origin, and the people we have met here. You must compare the generalizations we make with your experience as you become more familiar with the United States, and be prepared to discard our advice if it does not work for you.

We know that just as the wobbles and falls are quickly forgotten once you know how to ride a bicycle and are enjoying the experience, you will forget much of your adjustment experience as you become more skilled at living in the United States. But we would like to know if this book has helped you, and we would appreciate your suggestions on how we can improve it for future editions. Write to us at 1919 North Summit Avenue, 9C, Milwaukee, WI 53202.

Acknowledgments

Our thanks and appreciation are due to the many people who provided insight and interviews for this book. Writers Esther Wanning, Alison Lanier, Craig Storti, and Gary Althen, immigration attorney Niloufer Hai, Ted Napiorkowski of Milwaukee's International Institute, and many foreign students gave us valuable information in interviews. Judy Brodd, foreign student advisor at the University of Wisconsin-Milwaukee allowed us to observe her orientation session for foreign students. Paul McInerny of Marquette University, the Public Relations Department at Northwestern Mutual Life, and Martin Hintz of Hintz and Co. provided many of the photographs. For their support and facilitation, artist Carl Ruppert and Cecilia Gilbert of Milwaukee's Department of City Development deserve our thanks. We appreciated the assistance of the International Broadcasters of the Voice of America, Geeta Sharma-Jensen of the *Milwaukee Journal*, Dorothy Shattuck and her volunteers at the Hmong Methodist Church ESL program in Milwaukee, and the hosts of the ethnic radio shows on WYMS 88.9 FM. For their patience, we thank the librarians at the Milwaukee Public Library. And most of all, thanks to David Baldwin and Leonard Levine for their encouragement.

1 Preparation and Arrival

Perhaps you are in the United States to study at an American university or to visit family and friends. You may be working temporarily at a corporation located in the United States, or maybe you will make this country your own. Whether you are living in the United States for a few months or a few years, this book will guide you through the survival stage and help you with the basics of adjustment to life in America.

When you do not have the comfort of knowing you will soon be going back to familiar ways and customs and are on your way to life in a new land, you can prepare mentally and physically for your adventure by getting more information. The more prepared you are to deal with mundane details, the more energy you will have to spend on observing the people, customs, politics, and subtleties of American life.

The name you put on your papers will be your official personal name for your stay in the United States. Since changing it after arrival will be difficult, ask someone familiar with American English to advise you. Check spelling and meanings before making out your immigration materials.

Once you have made all the arrangements for work, study, immigration, and travel to the United States, get yourself an international driver's license (see Appendix). The rest of this chapter includes some tips to prepare you for your journey to the U.S.A. and the chaos, fun, excitement, and, sometimes, trauma of arrival.

PACKING AND DRESSING FOR YOUR JOURNEY
Try not to pack clothing that requires starch, crushes easily, or that requires special treatment to get clean. Pack in plastic bags anything that could spill or leak. Know the contents of your bags and be able to recognize

them immediately. It may be normal in your culture for a relative to pack luggage for you, but a U.S. official seeking narcotics smugglers is not likely to be sympathetic to any indication that you cannot recognize your baggage or are not sure of its contents. If anyone asks you to carry a parcel into the United States for them, open it to be certain of the contents before you agree to transport it.

If you wear glasses or contact lenses, carry your prescription with you. If you are taking any medication, ask your doctor to write a prescription for the composition, not the brand name sold in your country. Drugs that are legal in other countries are not always legal in the United States. Contact your local U.S. embassy or consulate for the most up-to-date customs and permit information.

Buy a luggage cart or travel light. You are entering a do-it-yourself economy where anything involving human labor is expensive. Men and women should wear comfortable, loose-fitting clothes that allow you to move quickly and efficiently to pick up your own bags. Wear comfortable, low-heeled shoes.

Carry your passport, your entry papers, complete name and address information for all the people you know in the United States, any correspondence with your expected place of work or study, and a detailed list of the contents of your baggage on your person. Place a copy of these documents in each bag as well. Mark your baggage clearly with your name and a U.S. address—even if it is a hotel.

If your home country has restrictions that allow you to take only personal jewelry out of the country, you may find that you have to wear a lot of valuables on your person to export the desired items. However, for safety, do not continue to wear all your jewelry; remove it before arrival in a major city.

If you have a long journey and any dietary restrictions, you might consider packing some fruit in your hand luggage, but be sure to finish eating it before arrival in the United States, since plants and plant products are not allowed into the country. U.S. electricity standards require that appliances operate on 110 volts and 60 cycles; step-down transformers are expensive and not widesy available. Currently, items manufactured in Cuba, North Korea, Kampuchea (Cambodia), and Vietnam may not be brought into the United States.

Make arrangements to have between $100 and $150 in cash (American currency) at a minimum when you arrive to avoid waiting in line at a bank counter to exchange your money. While there are no restrictions on how much money you may bring into the United States, your own country may have some regulations on the amount of money you may depart with. If you can take more with you, carry it in international traveler's checks.

WELCOME TO THE U.S.A.

If you arrive over the Canadian border, you may be surprised to find that very little looks different. The length of vowels increases, the pace of life increases, but the landscape and standard of living look the same. The differences between Canada and the United States are subtle: most are caused by the difference in political and economic systems. The United States is a place of higher risk than Canada, with correspondingly greater monetary reward. If you arrive over the Mexican border, the differences lie in language, industrialization, population, and standard of living and are immediately apparent.

If you travel by airplane and have to change planes in the United States to arrive at your final destination, verify with an airline employee that all your luggage is marked with the appropriate destination airport code. It is quite possible to arrive at your final destination before your luggage, even if you are traveling on a well-regarded airline. But don't panic. You can clear immigration in the first city you enter in the United States and clear customs at your final destination once your baggage arrives. If problems arise, the airline you traveled on from your original destination is responsible for tracing your luggage.

If you expect friends to greet you at the airport, the usual place to meet them will be outside the baggage claim area for your flight, after you have cleared immigration and customs. If you don't find your friends there, approach a Traveler's Aid volunteer or an airline official and ask them to "page" your friends (announce their names on the loudspeaker system) to tell them where to meet you.

If you are from a country where it is assumed that signs are for the occasional stranger, and the signs are thus few and inaccurate, you will have to force yourself to read and trust the signs and notices that are posted everywhere. Because of the tremendous mobility of the U.S. population, everyone operates on the assumption that the written word is likely to be more accurate than information from a human being. Don't stop people to confirm information written on notices; you are likely to be referred back to the notice.

Ask for help when you need it. If you do not ask for help, Americans will assume you do not need it. Do not expect people to see your need or notice distress from the way you look. Practice saying, "Could I ask you a favor?" and "Would you be able to help me?" An even more direct request, conveying greater urgency, would be, "How do I find. . .?" Expecting an American to come to the conclusion that you need help without stating it directly can result in a much longer conversation than necessary. In addition, you could find that the American misses the point, or becomes impatient, perceiving your indirectness to be a "game."

DEALING WITH BORDER OFFICIALS

Customs and immigration officials are ordinary people who have been given extraordinary power, as is the case anywhere in the world. Travelers report less "hassle" (trouble) from U.S. customs officials than from customs officials in many other countries because more items are allowed entry into the United States. In contrast, immigration officials are supposed to inspect your papers and, if necessary, exclude you from the United States. They must satisfy themselves that you are the person identified in your travel documents. Treat them with a healthy respect, but be aware that you have the right to maintain your dignity. Be prepared for some U.S.

Preparation and Arrival

officials to assert their authority by staying expressionless and being sensitive to the slightest infraction of any rules written on signs, particularly if you try to get ahead in a line (queue).

If your culture has taught you that looking people in the eye is disrespectful, we recommend that you break yourself of that assumption right away. Look an official in the eyes or at a spot between his or her eyebrows as you speak. If you have had problems entering the country before, don't say only what you think the immigration official would like to hear: tell the truth. Any previous record of problems with immigration is maintained on INS computers, is likely to be at the fingertips of any immigration official, and you're a long way from home.

There are many reasons for which a person may be refused entry to the United States. If you are a Muslim and you have more than one wife, be aware that you can be disqualified from entering the United States under the provision excluding polygamists. If you have been a member of a Communist party in your home country, you can be excluded. (This factor is likely to surprise newcomers unfamiliar with American history but aware of America's reputation for free speech and association.) Aliens who "are likely to become a public charge" are excludable, so be prepared to show papers to prove you have money or a sponsor who will support you. There are a number of other reasons, but we think these are the ones likely to be used in the next few years.

If you are excluded and find yourself under threat of deportation, know that you are protected by the U.S. Constitution and must be allowed a deportation "hearing" (where a judge hears your case), and "parole" (permission to stay) until that hearing. If it seems to you that the terms used imply that the Immigration Service operates under the assumption that they are dealing with people guilty until proven innocent, you are beginning to get the picture.

No matter what the border officials say or do, the best policy is to decide you will not be offended or insulted and to make up your mind that you will not let it affect your opinion of America, Americans, or human beings in general. Separate yourself from your country in your thinking, and refuse to let any disparagement of your country or countrymen by a border official reflect on you as an individual.

Once you are out of the hands of the border officials, breathe a sigh of relief and a prayer for the next person in line. Collect your baggage. Exchange some money at the bank if need be. Walk outside. Now you have truly arrived in the U.S.A.

FIRST IMPRESSIONS

Americans speak American, not English. This is not immediately apparent, as you are likely to be asked to speak English. And in the south of the country, they speak Southern—even though you will still be requested to "speak English"! It may take you a while to accustom yourself to the American way of talking, no matter how many American movies you have watched before arrival. Americans tend to speak louder to anyone they cannot understand, unconsciously assuming that volume alone will get the message through. This may look like anger to many newcomers, but it is actually quite harmless.

No matter what accent you bring with you (no one speaks "accentless" English or any other language), you may be able to make yourself more understandable to Americans by changing most of your *a*'s to *e*'s. For instance, you are likelier to be understood if you say "th*e*nk you" rather than "th*a*nk you," "b*e*n*e*na" rather than "b*a*n*a*na," "cl*e*ss" rather than "cl*a*ss," and "*e*sk" rather than "*a*sk." In the long run, you may find it beneficial to take some advanced conversational English lessons. Contact the voluntary agency listed in the Appendix that is closest to you to ask for information on English as a Second Language, or ESL, classes. While ESL classes offered by voluntary agencies are usually provided at no charge, universities and technical colleges in your city offer them as well for a small fee.

Taxicab (taxi or cab) drivers in most large American cities speak any language other than English. For some newcomers, an excellent way to get a quick lift of spirits on your first day is to ask the taxi dispatcher for a driver

Preparation and Arrival 7

American currency

from your home country. Ask the driver: Where are the shops owned by people from our home country? Where can one get food from our home country? Is there an expatriate TV show or radio program from our home country in this town? Even if you never use the answers to these questions, they play an important part in raising your confidence.

Be careful as you pay the cab driver. American money denominations all look alike: the currency is green. A $20 bill can be easily mistaken for a $10 bill. You might end up giving a larger tip than you intended. American coins are a little confusing, too: a 5-cent coin (called a nickel) is larger than a 10-cent coin (called a dime). A 25-cent coin is called a quarter because it is a quarter of a dollar. A popular slang expression for a dollar bill ($1) is a "buck." The 1-cent copper coin is called a penny.

The overwhelming impression of most newcomers is that of being in a land of plenty. Food is very cheap, even when you make calculations to convert prices into your home currency, and every store is stocked to overflowing with goods—some with items you may consider luxuries or superfluous. But look closer. There are beggars on the streets of major cities and long lines outside government job-service offices. America is at a stage right now where it is becoming necessary to deal with the issue of scarcity, something other cultures have adjusted to generations ago. Until you have some idea of the purchasing power of American money, conserve your funds and look at several different sources before you buy. This is called "shopping around."

If the area of the United States that you arrive in has a very different landscape from the one you are used to, be prepared for a feeling that the land is ugly. If you are used to hills and your surroundings are flat so that you can see for miles, or if you are used to tropical climates and find yourself in a part of the United States where it snows, it can be years, some newcomers tell us, before you begin to feel that your surroundings could be called beautiful.

If you come from a less industrialized country, you may find that the lack of natural textures in America causes a constant feeling of unreality. When everything you touch has an unfamiliar feel because you encounter more man-made textures than you are accustomed to, try carrying a piece of wood or a stone in your pocket. It is amazing how much comfort this can bring; you are, after all, on the same planet.

MEETING AMERICANS

Your first encounter with Americans will probably be in shops and restaurants where you are a customer, so you are likely to make this assessment: Americans smile. This first impression is one that many newcomers notice immediately, no matter where they come from. Not only do Americans smile but they also seem very friendly and willing to talk to anyone. But you need to place this in proper perspective, so you do not have a situation in which you believe you have made a new friend and the other person does not. Most companies train their employees that the customer is to be dealt with pleasantly, with regard for your time and in the hope that you will spend your money at their establishment. However, the quickest way to turn an American smile to a frown is to expect servility rather than pleasantry; for instance, do not snap your fingers to get the attention of a waiter or waitress in a restaurant.

People will even smile when you ask them where the nearest toilet, washroom, or bathroom is. Every American restaurant must have a toilet or bathroom associated with it, so if you need to find a place in a hurry, head for the nearest restaurant. Marked with pictures or writing, facilities are separate for men and women unless the term "rest room" (often written "restroom") is used, in which case it could be a one-person facility used by one individual at a time. Hot-water faucets (taps) are marked "H" and are always to your left, even on one-lever fixtures. Cold water faucets are marked "C" and are on your right. Some newer washrooms have spouts and hand dryers that turn on and off in response to a person's motion opposite them. Watch what others do, and follow their example.

Most areas of the world today have fewer restrictions on smoking in public than you will find in America. If you would like to smoke, be careful to do it in a "Smoking Allowed" area only, and find an ashtray beforehand.

Take our word for it, all Americans do not really look alike. Not everyone has blond hair and blue eyes, either. In fact, America is a nation of nationalities; every country and every race is represented. But until your senses adjust to your new surroundings, you may find your eyes telling you that everyone looks the same. This can make it difficult to associate names and faces. Ask for a business card from anyone you would like to maintain contact with, or get contact information in writing.

Americans usually have two personal names and a family name (surname or last name). If you come from a country where this is not customary, you will need to fit your name into this format. A common irritant to newcomers from more formal societies is the immediate use of your name in conversation without any courtesy titles. Americans reserve "Mr." for people in high places (as in "Mr. President" or "Mr. Ambassador"). Women are likely to be addressed by first name in conversation and as "Ms." (pronounced *miz*), meaning simply "female person," in correspondence. "Sir" and "Ma'am" (pronounced *mam*) are commonly used by people serving customers and by younger people addressing older people in the southern part of the country.

Americans greet one another by saying "Hello" or "Hi, how are you?" The correct response is "Hi, how are *you*?" The first person is then expected to answer "Pretty good," or "Fine," or "OK." Then you move on to the purpose of the conversation. No one truly wants or needs to know how you are; if they do, the question is likely to be rephrased as, "How have you been?" or, "Are you doing OK?"

American equivalents for "Au revoir" are "See you later," "Bye, now," "Take care," or the overused "Have a nice day." We should caution newcomers that a lack of conversation—silence— can be an indication of rejection, nonparticipation, or a desire for privacy among casual acquaintances but is usually a sign of great comfort between old friends.

The farther your home country from the United States, the likelier you are to perceive that Americans smell different. Do not make the mistake of equating "different" with "bad". You probably smell as different to Americans as they do to you. The reason is simple: your diet is probably different. As you begin to eat American food, you will begin to smell like an American.

As in any country, you will find helpful people and not very helpful people, honest people and dishonest people, people who have high status and people who have low status, people who enjoy change and people who dislike change intensely, people who have a lot of money and people who do not have a lot of money. You are going to meet them all, but you may need to change a few assumptions to recognize who's who. For instance, it does not necessarily follow in America that people who have expensive clothes or a fancy car will be refined, educated, and sophisticated. Changing this assumption could prevent disappointment. Another assumption that does not hold in America is that interest in, and access to, cultural activities such as classical music, theater, or fine arts is restricted to those with money.

America is a great experiment in having a world without borders and nationalities. If your home country has a racially homogeneous population, it can come as a shock to find that in daily life in America you need to deal with people of other races. Some may be the very people your country considered enemies.

You may find yourself having to adjust from being a majority member of your home-country population to being a minority member in America, perhaps with correspondingly less power and lower status. Remember that you bring with you the stereotypes you have been raised with—every culture has its own racism—but an asset you have as a newcomer is that you are not likely to have internalized stereotypes about races and peoples your culture has never encountered. Try not to learn any stereotypes from mainstream Americans. Observe and make up your own mind.

All this does not mean you should trust everyone you meet. There are people who will take advantage of newcomers, just as in your home country. Stay in well-lighted public areas. Do not give your passport or entry papers to anyone other than an immigration official or a foreign student advisor. Do not get on an elevator (lift) alone with anyone who looks suspicious. Walk as if you know where you are going even if you do not. Do not take a ride with anyone "going your way." If you are a female newcomer, try not to take a taxi alone; take any form of public or semipublic transportation, such as an airport bus or multipassenger automobile, that goes to downtown hotels.

Be ready to make a noise or run if you find yourself threatened in any way. If someone tries to rob you, remember your life is more valuable than money or jewelry. (To protect your jewelry, rent a "safety deposit box" in a bank.)

At this point, you are likely to be separated from your family and everyone who knows you and your past. For some, this brings a heady sense of freedom and release. For others, it brings a feeling of great apprehension. We have some tips:

- Do not do anything you would have been ashamed to do in your home environment.
- Strangers are friends we have not yet met.
- Remember that fear is the greatest barrier to communication.

The best way to get rid of apprehension is to get more information.

EVALUATING SOURCES OF INFORMATION IN AMERICA

As a newcomer you will encounter many individuals and institutions, each offering advice. In fact, America is a country where one can easily get a bad case of "information overload." Under the barrage of information a newcomer experiences, it is tempting to trust only the individuals or institutions you know or that are similar to the ones in the old country. Both of these courses of action are inadvisable if you wish to survive in America and maximize the possibilities that it has to offer. Instead, the first step to survival is to examine, evaluate, and, if need be, change your definition of "authoritative" information. Here is how Americans evaluate sources of information in a country where too much information rather than too little is the problem.

In many countries, it is assumed that any older person, a man, or anything in print gives authoritative information. In the United States, this assumption is not made. First of all, not everything you see in print, not everything you hear on the radio, and certainly not everything you see on television is the truth. Freedom of expression is allowed, so that everyone has a chance to make up his or her own mind about what to believe. That means that any opinion can be expressed publicly except for something clearly dangerous such as yelling "Fire!" in a crowded theater. At the same time, anything and everything can be questioned for accuracy.

In entering new and different situations, most Americans respect the opinions of other people who (1) are in similar situations at present, (2) have experienced the same situation, or (3) have written or spoken about it in published form or in a public forum. American journalists are more inclined to omit news facts than to misstate the facts. The best defense is to read widely and eclectically. Our evaluation of print and broadcast information sources is given in the Appendix.

We advise you to trust your own judgment in light of your own aspirations. This is the fastest way to learn and the surest way to survive.

A FEW DETAILS

All immigrants and most nonimmigrants are required to be registered and fingerprinted at the closest INS office or police station. Do not overlook this process, even if it makes you feel like a common felon.

You need a Social Security number to work in the United States and for many other areas of American life, as many organizations use it as an identifier. Get one as soon as you can. You can apply for a Social Security number at any Social Security office; call 1-800-234-5772 to find the one nearest you.

Social Security is a retirement plan whose benefits are available to noncitizens who have worked in covered employment in the United States for a certain period of time. Your employer must deduct a contribution to this plan from your paycheck even if you plan to be in the United States for less time than the qualification period and never expect to receive benefits from it. You are eligible to receive Social Security benefit payments if you have paid into the plan while working in the U.S.A. and are still in the country when you retire or become disabled.

2 Dining Out

Outdoor eating places you will encounter include sidewalk cafés and sidewalk vendors, whose food is periodically checked by city inspectors for sanitary handling and is generally clean and wholesome. There are many and varied indoor eating establishments in the United States, and there are numerous customs related to each.

COMMERCIAL DINING PLACES

The term "restaurant" is used for a large variety of eating places; smaller is not always cheaper. In general, white tablecloths and serving staff indicate higher prices and fancier food. Fifteen percent is the usual tip. You must be over 21 years of age in most states to be served alcoholic beverages.

In fast-food restaurants, such as McDonald's, taking home napkins or plastic utensils or packages of condiments, such as mustard or ketchup, left on the counter for customers is not considered correct behavior. The store owner has paid for these items, and you would be stealing not only from the owner but from all the other diners as the price of the food will eventually be raised to cover the loss.

"Take-out" places will prepare food in advance if you call them on the phone. You then pick up and pay for the food and take it home to eat. Delicatessens (known as "delis"), Chinese food, or pizza restaurants will have take-out or delivery service.

CAFETERIAS

Universities and corporations often have cafeterias, large rooms with a long buffet counter at one end. Typically, you are expected to take a tray, perhaps a soup bowl, cutlery (also called utensils), and napkins from one end of the counter and stand in line. The line moves past a selection of food items, some of which are hot and some of which are cold. Workers behind the counter serve you

Dining Out

Taking out food at a fast-food restaurant (Photo courtesy McDonald's Corporation)

hot food items, but you are expected to serve yourself the cold ones.

You are expected to be quick in deciding what you would like to eat, so as not to cause people in the line behind you to wait. Sometimes this is difficult when the foods are unfamiliar or when you need more information before you can decide of the food is correct for you to eat. Our suggestion is to look at the food, read the menu if it is written above the buffet, read the prices, and make your decisions before you get in line.

At the end of the line you will usually find a cashier who will tell you what the items you have selected will cost you. If the total comes to more than you planned, it is perfectly acceptable to ask if you can leave one or more of the cold items with the cashier rather than spend more than your budget allows. You are not expected to return the items to their original locations; leave them with the cashier. Cashiers sometimes have tip jars next to them. You may tip them, but no one will think any less of you if you do not.

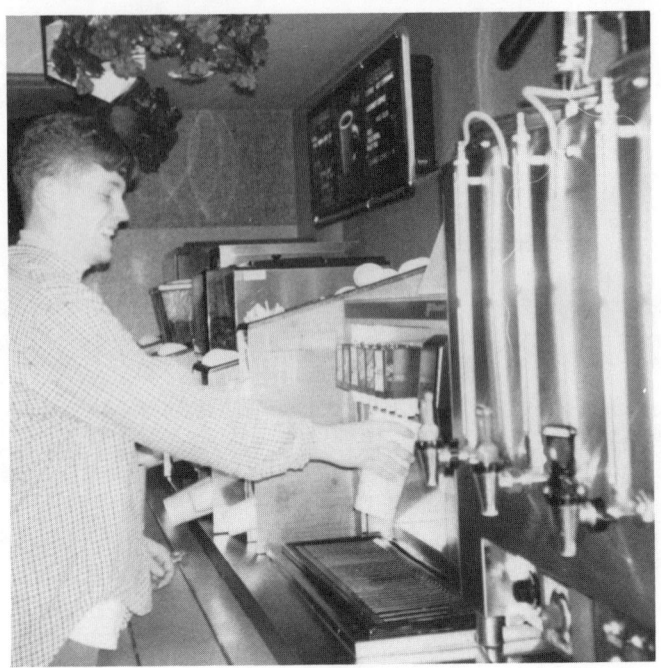

In a cafeteria (Photo by Shauna Singh Baldwin)

MEAL PLANS FOR COLLEGE STUDENTS

If you are coming to the United States to attend college, most colleges will send you information about meal plans well in advance of your arrival. A meal plan is a system in which you pay the university or its catering service a sum of money in advance, and when you arrive at school, it is up to you to claim the card or packet of coupons or ticket that allows you to eat at the university cafeteria or dining room every mealtime.

Some universities make this a requirement for first-year students (freshmen), so that they meet and get to know one another. The advantage to the university is that it gets a sum of money in the beginning of the semester, making it easier for the catering service to plan for each meal.

If you have a choice, you should ask yourself a few questions before you agree to purchase a meal plan. Will you use it often enough to justify the cost? This question

Dining Out

leads to more questions. How far away is the cafeteria from where you plan to live? If the cafeteria is some distance from your dormitory or apartment, will you make the effort to go to it, or will you find yourself buying snacks to munch on in your room? One reason to purchase a meal plan is that it forces you to be with people while you are undergoing "culture shock." If you find yourself withdrawing from people, you may need an additional incentive to maintain a friendly outgoing attitude during this adjustment.

BARS AND NIGHTCLUBS

Depending on your country of origin, you may have some reservations about frequenting places where alcoholic beverages are the primary focus. Called saloons, pubs, taverns, bars, or nightclubs depending on the region of the country and their price range, these establishments have sometimes been portrayed by the movies as decadent. You may enjoy going to taverns, bars, or nightclubs even if you do not drink alcoholic beverages. Many taverns and nightclubs have a distinctive culture;

In a bar (Photo by Jane Gleeson)

nightclubs, by definition, offer entertainment, which can range from exotic dancing to poetry reading. Some are cozy places to sit and "people-watch" and to learn from cultural interaction. Others are "singles bars" where a partner you find could become your mate. Still others are places where it is assumed you are looking for a sex partner.

Often, taverns are places where it is common for men to drink or eat alone. (Women are likelier to choose a family restaurant if they find it necessary to eat alone.) Tipping is expected at bars. Do not assume that a waiter or waitress is "available" merely because he or she works in a tavern or nightclub. Always treat people with respect if you wish to be treated with respect.

DINING AT SOMEONE'S HOME

American dinner invitations tend to be scheduled in advance. When you are invited, you are expected, in this era of time pressure, to consider the time your host spends with you a true compliment and a generous gesture. Unless it is a Saturday evening invitation, your host or hostess will have to cook and clean up and then go to work early the next morning. This is easy to forget if you come from a country where work begins later in the day or if you have an impression that all Americans are rich and therefore have hired help.

A family meal at the home of a friend of the same gender is an event that indicates friendship regardless of the opinion of other family members. A family meal at the home of a person of the opposite sex, however, can sometimes take on unanticipated aspects of "meet the family in preparation for marriage." You should make it extremely clear that the occasion signals no romantic attachment unless that is indeed the case.

"Dinner" is the main meal, eaten after work in cities, at noon in country areas. "Lunch" is a noontime meal in cities. If unsure about the time you are expected to arrive, ask your host or hostess rather than guess and be wrong. It is better to be on time than late. Some people will expect you to telephone if you will be even 10 minutes late. Bringing flowers with you is a nice gesture but not required.

Dining Out

If there are certain things you do not or cannot eat, it is best to tell your host what they are at the time the invitation is extended. You will be expected to taste the food served, but you do not have to eat what is served if you had no control over what was put on your plate. If something is served that you do not recognize, it is better to ask what it is made of than to eat it and be unhappy.

If a cocktail or wine is served before the meal but you do not drink alcoholic beverages, it is better to ask for plain water, soda water, fruit juice, or a "soft drink" such as a Coke than to decline to partake of any beverage.

Some people say "grace," a blessing before eating. If you are not of the same religion as your host, the best way for you to behave is to sit quietly until grace is finished and eat when others begin to eat.

If you do not like the food that is served, or if you have a dietary restriction that prevents you from eating it, your hosts will not be offended if you politely decline a dish without revealing any judgment of those who choose to eat it. Remember, however, that in America if you decline an opportunity (and this applies to more than food), you may not be asked twice. It is assumed that you know the needs of your body best, and no one will watch to ensure that you do not go away hungry.

Sometimes meals are served "family style," which means that large serving bowls will be used for each type of food. You are expected to take a small portion for yourself and put it on your plate, then pass the serving bowl to the next person on either your left or right. The bowl is not to be eaten from directly.

Men and women eat at the same table at the same time, and your male host is likely to assist in serving. Conversation by both men and women is expected and encouraged during meals.

An American "party" is generally confined to one age group. Birthday parties for children, for example, will rarely include adults except as chaperones. Cocktail parties are usually attended by adults within a ten-year range of ages. Graduation parties are only for the graduate and his or her friends; parental age individuals are expected to be invisible. In contrast, "barbecues" and "brunches" are occasions when you are likely to meet people of varying ages.

BARBECUES
An outdoor barbecue or Bar-B-Q (to give it its Wild West name) is also referred to as a "cookout." It is usually a long lazy affair held in someone's large backyard or at a public park. Starting early when people get to the park or gathering place and finishing when the weather changes or the food is finished or when people are too full to talk any more, barbecues are generally reserved for informal entertaining. The group will make a fire in a grill (barbecue grill) and cook such things as steak, patties of ground beef (hamburgers), or chicken or pork sausage on top. After it is cooked, the meat is served with cold salads, baked beans, or vegetables. The meal is usually served on disposable paper plates so that no cleaning is required. Alcoholic beverages may be served before and with the food. It is appropriate for a guest to offer to bring a salad or dessert of some sort and to assist with the cleaning up, rather than expecting the host or hostess to do it all. It is traditional for men to be the cooks at a barbecue while women do the cleanup.

BRUNCHES
A brunch is a meal midway between breakfast and lunch (hence the word "brunch"), served either late in the morning or at midday, usually Saturday or Sunday, that combines a breakfast and lunch menu. Eggs and ham or bacon or dishes combining these are popular, served with cold salads and followed by dessert(s). Orange juice or punch served at these events is often mixed with champagne. As with a barbecue, it is appropriate for a guest to offer to bring a salad or dessert of some sort and to assist with the cleaning up. Brunch is often served on Sundays at hotels and community centers as well and is nearly always an excellent value for the money.

SOME MINOR POINTS
If your custom has been to eat without use of fork and knife, watch people around you; it is not difficult.

A typical American table setting

American custom is to hold the knife in the right hand, fork in the left, cut the food on the plate, and then transfer the fork to the right hand to eat. European custom keeps the knife in the right hand, fork in the left, with no transfer. Both are acceptable.

When in a fine restaurant or at a formal dinner where several knives, forks, and spoons are laid at each person's plate, the rule to use is "Start from the outside and work your way in," allowing one set of utensils for each course. It is a social blunder to lick your knife in public (children are always being told this), but be sure to "four o'clock the silverware" when you are finished. This means placing fork and knife together slanting 45 degrees to the right of the center of the plate to indicate you are finished eating even if there is food left on the plate.

Coffee is served before, during, and after meals in America. If you are a tea drinker, here are some options to consider as you adjust to this land of coffee drinkers. You can:

1. Ask for tea. You will be served a cup or small pot of hot or tepid water, a tea bag, usually a wedge of lemon, and perhaps some honey. Most restaurants offer a choice of herbal or other kinds of teas and charge by the cup or pot.

2. Carry your own tea bags, tea leaves, and spices, as desired, with you. Then all you have to do is ask for hot water. In restaurants, you may be asked to pay for a cup of tea anyway as a charge for the service.

3. Switch to coffee. American coffee is considered quite weak by many newcomers, but "espresso" or "Turkish" coffee can be ordered at many restaurants in large cities. Most restaurants offer you a choice between "regular" coffee (with caffeine) and "decaf" coffee (decaffeinated, or without caffeine). Your cup will be filled, or "warmed up," until you ask the server to stop.

3 Communicating

The United States has a highly verbal culture. If you do not speak, people may assume your silence indicates rejection of them or their ideas, or even arrogance, though it may also be interpreted as shyness. Even listening is expected to be an active state in which the listener assures the speaker at intervals that he or she is still listening, by saying "Yes" or "Uh-huh" or nodding.

Get used to giving and receiving compliments. Americans use compliments as ways to give each other moral support in a highly fragmented world and as ways to open conversations. If you are complimented, accept the compliment with a "Thank you." You are not expected to protest unless it is obviously untrue. But if you want the conversation to continue, you should follow the thanks with a comment on the subject.

Americans have an orientation that moves from the specific to the general, not, as in other cultures, from general statements to specific observations. An American may begin a conversation with a specific detail and the general idea is situated at the end of the conversation. This can be a little irritating if your orientation is the opposite.

Try not to interrupt. Americans do not treat interruptions as an attempt to give equal time to participants in a conversation but as rude attempts to dominate the person who was interrupted. However, you have the corresponding right to talk without interruption. After a few years here, you may even find yourself using a phrase you might initially consider very impolite: "Let me finish."

Americans assume that talking about anything that bothers you is healthy, so one of the qualities most valued in a friend is the capacity to listen. This assumption can lead to situations in which you find you are expected to talk about things you consider personal, while the American is merely showing friendship. If someone asks you a question you would rather not answer, you can always say, "If you don't mind, I'd rather not answer that" or "I'm sorry, that's a hard question for me to answer."

Conversations can begin with "small talk" and then turn to more serious and important topics. After the weather, the most common topic is work. People ask "What do you do?" which means "What is your job?" or "Where do you work (or study)?" Plans for weekend and vacation activities are popular topics, followed by family. People ask questions like, "What does your husband/wife do?" or "Where does your husband/wife work?"

Be careful not to assume that American values are the same as those of your home culture. For instance, ask, "Do you have children?" not "When are you going to have children?" And because of the large number of cohabiting couples in America, it is more polite to ask, "Are you married to one another?" instead of assuming it. Never say, "When are you going to get married to one another?" The words *should* and *ought* are expected to be used only by people who write books like this one or by one's own parents. So try not to say, "You should have another child" or "You ought not to drop out of school." If you feel the need to make a suggestion, use the more American "You might want to. . ." or "Perhaps you could. . ."

Use the phrase "In my country we. . ." sparingly, only when you need to explain a misunderstanding. If used too often, you are likely to meet the response, "Well, you're not in your country now."

Do not be surprised if your idea of what is funny and what Americans think is funny are very different. What is important in your adjustment stage is to try to determine whether someone is laughing *with* you or *at* you. A person laughing with you is trying to establish a basis of friendship. Unless the speaker is unmistakably specific, do not interpret a comment made about you personally as being made about your entire country. If you feel someone has laughed at you, you should talk about it with that person. Silence is not enough. But if the comment was about all people from your country, tell the speaker how it made you feel and let him or her know you will not tolerate such comments.

Americans usually look for similarities, things they have "in common" with people when they meet them. Often the way similarities are established is by discussing television shows, music, and movies they have recently enjoyed (books are rarely discussed with strangers). You cannot be expected to be familiar with American television series, old songs, or old movies. Even if you have seen them, they will not have made the same impact on you as on an American. This is not always obvious to Americans. It is sometimes effective to point out to anyone who considers this a symptom of ignorance (or worse, backwardness) that there are many songs, actors, films, and television series in your home country that Americans have "missed out on."

The following phrases are used as ways to end a conversation and have no meaning beyond that: "See you later," "I'll call you," "We really must get together." If people truly wish to see one another again, they make an appointment or call one another on the telephone.

THE TELEPHONE

America's telephone system works, and its reliability is legendary. The American telephone industry is not, as is the case in most countries, owned by the government. Instead, there are about 1,500 local telephone companies in the United States and about 14 long-distance companies. Each one publishes a telephone directory that gives you instructions on how to make local, long-distance, and international calls. The instructions are easy to follow if you know that there is no + symbol on the telephone; the "plus sign" between numerals is only for logical separation.

Telephone manners vary a great deal within the country. The general practice is for the person answering the telephone to speak first, saying "Hello," then to wait for the calling party to speak. A safe and easy way to ensure that you give a good impression when you answer the telephone at work is to say "Hello" and introduce yourself, giving your first and last names. If you come from a country where your last name is expected to precede your first name, you can answer the telephone that way, but be prepared to explain later what you wish to be called.

If one American calls another, there is usually some reason for calling stated early in the conversation. (This, of course, is a rule that does not apply to teenagers.) Because Americans consider a telephone call an intrusion that cannot be ignored, it is not considered polite to call a person's home before 8:00 a.m. or after 9:00 p.m. unless you have permission. It is not considered impolite to tell the caller that he or she is calling at an inconvenient time and to arrange for a mutually convenient time for the conversation to take place.

Telephone answering machines, however, have no time schedule. It seems sometimes that Americans all call and leave messages for one another on answering machines and do not talk directly to each other any more. So it is important to leave messages that sound as if you are talking directly to the person you want to reach, not to a machine. If you have your own answering machine, try to make your greeting message clear and simple. Some answering machines are equipped with the capability to record conversations. Be aware, however, that it is against the law to record a conversation without the consent of the other party to the conversation.

Being very conscious of time and desirous of making every moment productive, Americans tend to start a business conversation by stating the purpose of the call, dealing with the issue at hand, and then, perhaps, branching into other subjects. Do not be annoyed if you have spent the weekend with an American and his or her whole family and you get a call on Monday in which no reference is made to the weekend until the business issue is resolved. Many Americans would want to establish right away that the personal relationship does not in any way compromise their objectivity when it comes to business.

It is accepted practice to make large and important

Using a pay telephone (Photo by Shauna Singh Baldwin)

commitments to people on the telephone; Americans consider it unnecessary to meet in person to ratify a telephone agreement. However, it is perfectly acceptable to request that a verbal commitment be ratified in writing after a business conversation or for one of the parties to the conversation to write a letter that confirms the content of the conversation.

Do not make a commitment to call someone unless you intend to do so or you wish to have no further business with that person. If someone has promised to call you and does not, it is that person who is being rude; it is rarely anything you have done.

Remember that the United States has four time zones, so that when it is noon in New York, it is 9:00 a.m. in California. If you are making a long-distance call, consult the area code and time zone information at the front of the telephone directory before you disturb anyone too early or too late in *their* day.

Using the Telephone Directory

American telephone directories have two major sections in smaller cities and towns and two kinds of "telephone books" in larger cities. "White Pages" list home or individual numbers and addresses as well as businesses and organizations alphabetically; and "Yellow Pages" list only commercial or business telephone numbers and addresses categorized by service provided or product sold. Many telephone books also include a "government" section that has numbers of city, county, state, and federal or national government offices listed separately.

Yellow Page telephone directory

The index at the beginning of the Yellow Pages book is the place to start if you want to find out where you can buy a certain item. If the word you are using to describe the item is not what the telephone book uses, in most cases you will be referred to the correct category. If in doubt, ask an operator by using the 0 button on the telephone. Although the Yellow Page directory groups businesses by product or service provided, sometimes there is an additional section that presents businesses by geographic location or by any other category required to help customers find them easily. For example, to find a restaurant whose name you know, look alphabetically under R for Restaurants, then under the name of the individual establishment. To find a restaurant in a particular area of the city or by type of food offered, use additional listings following the alphabetical one.

Directory assistance operators can help you locate a person or a business with a new listing (number) or a new address. There is a charge for this service. Unpublished or unlisted numbers, however, will not be revealed even by this operator.

Your nearest library may have another book, called a "city directory," which can help you locate a business or personal telephone number when all you can remember is the street the person lives on or the business address of the store you once bought something from. In larger cities, this service is often provided by telephone and free of charge by the library.

Rights and Responsibilities of a Telephone Subscriber
As a "subscriber" paying for the use of a residential telephone, you have a right to correct billing, to good quality lines, and to assistance when you need it. Complaints are expected and indeed, welcomed—in contrast to telephone companies in other countries. The assumption is that service cannot improve unless the company knows that the existing service is not meeting a customer's standard of excellence.

You have a right to request that the telephone company shall not sell your number and address to direct mail marketing companies, but the information about your payment history belongs to them and is salable to, for instance, credit bureaus.

You can call your long-distance telephone company and request rate information before making a call, so that you do not spend beyond your budget. If you find, however, that you are not able to meet your telephone expenses, contact your local telephone company immediately and work out a payment plan. They bill on behalf of long-distance companies as well, so you may not have to deal with two creditors. Do not evade the issue or stall. It is best to "tell it like it is," and you will be respected for your candor.

Telephone calling cards issued by the telephone company should not be used by anyone but the person to whom they are issued. Using someone else's card and personal identification code without their knowledge is prohibited by law and easy for the telephone company to trace. Americans also consider it highly unethical.

THE POST OFFICE
The U.S. Post Office is a quasi-governmental agency. That means it is a federal, or national-level, government agency not totally supported by tax dollars. It must pay its own way from the money it collects by selling postage stamps and postal service. In contrast to many other countries, the U.S. Postal Service is a rather efficient enterprise, although you will not find many Americans who think so. It provides a wide variety of services, including Selective Service (draft) registration of young males over the age of 18 (whether citizens or not) and mailbox rental for people whose addresses change faster than the seasons. Addressing your letters in the way that post office mail sorters and sorting machines expect them to be addressed can often save your letter from delay or misdirection.

Addressing a Letter
The illustration below shows a sample of a correctly addressed domestic letter. Always use your return address. It may be placed either on the upper left-hand corner of the front of the envelope or on the flap of the envelope on the back. If a street name is to be complete, it should have the correct direction designation abbreviation (N., E., W., S.), if required, and correct street

```
Ms. Jane Brown
3456 Return Place
Return City, WI  53151-1502                    Stamp


              Mr. John Doe
              1234 W. Anyplace Rd., Apt. 1A
              Anytown, WI  53151-1502
```

A domestic envelope, correctly addressed

A mailbox (Photo by Shauna Singh Baldwin)

description abbreviation (St., Ave., Rd., Dr., Pl.). The apartment number for a residence or the office number for a business may be placed either after the street address or on the lower left-hand corner of the face of the envelope.

State names should be abbreviated using the official U.S. Post Office two-letter abbreviation printed in capital letters, such as WI for Wisconsin. Always use the 5-digit zip (postal) code. If you know the extended zip + 4 code, please use it. This is especially important for business letters.

Letters with correct postage may be mailed in any officially designated U.S. Post Office box (usually painted blue) on the street, inside a building, in a drive-up location, or at the post office or handed to any U.S. Post Office mail carrier. All of these methods are safe; you do not have to personally witness stamp cancellation.

Stamps can be purchased for their face value at U.S. Post Offices, at officially designated mail "substations" or coin-operated machines in commercial locations. You can order stamps by mail from the U.S. Post Office; inquire about this service. Some private mailing services and coin-operated machines, such as those found in hotels, will charge more than the price of the postage for the convenience of buying the stamps at that site.

What Is Allowed in the Mail
The U.S. Post Office will not accept mail that is not allowed by the country to which it is being sent. Domestic mail (mail within the United States) is handled by size and weight. Postcards should be a minimum of 5½ inches long by 3½ inches high, a maximum of 6 by 4¼ inches. Business letters generally are folded in thirds and enclosed in standard business-size envelopes, called "number 10" envelopes in office supply stores, which measure 9½ inches by 4⅛ inches. Larger envelopes require additional postage by size and weight. They may be weighed on any reliable scale before mailing or by the personnel at the post office before postage is affixed. Personal letters cannot be smaller than 5 inches long by 3½ inches high or less than .007 inch thick. Overseas mail fold-it letter forms, called "Aerogrammes," can be purchased at most larger post offices but are too thin to be used domestically.

You can mail tape cassettes in padded envelopes, computer floppy disks in special disk mailers, and medical X-rays in special envelopes, but you cannot ordinarily mail matches, flammable liquids, or dead animals. Trying to mail a prohibited item if you really must do so involves special permission from the postmaster in charge. Parcels must be wrapped securely by the sender, using brown paper wrapping material (cut-up grocery bags are perfectly acceptable) or stronger materials and sealed with gummed-paper tape, string, nails, screws, wire, or metal bands as required. The purpose of this kind of seal is to allow detection of tampering during shipment. Never send cash, a bearer check, a demand draft, a cashier's check, a bearer bond, or jewelry as ordinary mail. Such valuables may be sent by registered mail for an additional fee (insured if you choose); this means you will receive a "return receipt" showing the signature of the recipient.

Sending Mail Overseas
There are three main categories of international mail: LC mail, an abbreviation of the French words *lettres* and *cartes* (letters and cards); AO mail, for the French *autres objects* (other objects), which includes regular printed matter, books and sheet music, braille and tapes for the blind, small packets, and publisher's periodicals; and CP mail, an abbreviation for the French words *colis postaux*, meaning parcel post.

The illustration below shows a sample of a correctly addressed international LC mail letter. International letters may be addressed in languages that do not use the Roman alphabet if followed on a separate line by the city, district or province, and country name in Roman block capital letters. The entire return address should be in Roman letters or in English.

```
Mr. John Brown
3456 Return Place                          Stamp
Return City, WI 53151-1502
U.S.A.

              Jacques Moliere
              Rue de Champaign, Apt. 3068
              06570 St. Paul
              FRANCE
```

An international envelope, correctly addressed

Sending Parcels Overseas
Surface parcel post and air parcel post (CP mail) may both be mailed at U.S. Post Offices, with insurance and return receipts if desired. In general, two to four pounds is about the right weight for parcel post packages. Air

parcel post rates for a one-pound package make it advantageous to send packages that size by air. Naturally, the greater the weight, the higher the cost. The crossover for surface shipment tends to be between four and five pounds; that is, as a "rule of thumb," if the package is under five pounds, send it by air; if it is over five pounds, use surface parcel post unless speed is very important and you are willing to pay the price for air parcel post.

Overnight Mail
Overnight mail, direct city-to-city air mail with delivery guaranteed by 10:00 a.m. the next day, costs a lot but is sometimes the only way to meet deadlines. The U.S. Post Office offers this service, but since it is not a monopoly, there are several alternatives, such as Federal Express (Fed Ex) and United Parcel Service (UPS).

Overnight mail is handled by size and weight. An overnight "letter" is really a flat package designed to ship up to 30 sheets of ordinary 8½-by-11-inch correspondence paper. No cash or valuables should be sent this way. Packages up to 2 pounds in weight can also be sent by overnight mail using "parcel paks."

"Next day" and "second day" delivery is also available from most shippers at lower costs. Rapid international service is offered by the U.S. Post Office, Federal Express, UPS, and DHL Worldwide Services, to name a few.

SENDING A TELEGRAM
You can send a telegram by using your telephone. This is called a "phoned telegram," and your message will sometimes be delivered by telephone. In America, the telegram has lost all connotation of urgency. One sometimes gets a telegram by regular mail, and it is often accompanied by a request from the telephone company for one's fax number or electronic mail address. This can be difficult to explain to people sending you telegrams from overseas in case of emergency. We recommend that you ask people overseas to use P.O.T.S. (plain old telephone service) for emergencies.

4 Getting Around

Keep your address and telephone number in your wallet or purse at all times. Always have the name, address, and telephone number of your destination written down for every trip you take, even a short one. If you come from a locality where everyone knows their neighbors, you might assume that in America you can stop anyone in the area and they will know the person you are looking for. People move so much in the United States that even people who want to help you find your friend or relative cannot do so without an address.

MAPS AND TRANSIT ROUTES

Psychological research has shown that we all carry around in our heads a "map" of where important geologic features are in relation to the place we grew up. We tend to stick to these maps like glue even in the face of experience that says the particular situation is different from our expectations. For example, if there was a large river or lake or other body of water to the east of the center of our hometown, we will, subconsciously, expect an equivalent body of water in our new area, even though there is no body of water at all or there is one, but in reality it is west of the center of town. What you have to do now is adjust to your new physical location as a whole as quickly as possible.

The first thing to do is get a map of the city and spend time studying it. Bookstores and gas stations sell detailed maps; free but not detailed maps are available at traveler's aid desks, visitor information bureaus, or a foreign student advisor's office. Wall-size maps are often on display in transportation centers, government offices, public schools, or libraries. Note the major geologic features: lakes, mountains, rivers, deserts. Are they east or west, north or south of the geographic center of town? People will give you two kinds of directions: turn left, turn right, or go east, or west, or north, or south. You are expected to know which direction is east or south. If you do not remember, do not be afraid to ask.

Most big cities have specialized areas with distinctive names. The primary shopping area is usually given a distinctive name (for example, downtown, the mall, or Broadway). This is also true of the primary business and financial district (for example, Wall Street, the City). Learn to associate informal, everyday names of sections with street names and official names of city areas.

Ask people: Where is "downtown," or is it called "uptown" or "city center"? How many shopping malls are there, or is "the mall" just one place? Where is "the depot," "the airport," or "the terminal"? How many of each are there? Where is "city hall"? "The courthouse"? Where do the wealthiest live? The poorest? Where do they shop? Where do middle-class families live? Where do they shop? Where do their children go to school? Where do artists live? Build your own map inside your head as you get to know your new city well.

Most U.S. cities are laid out on a mathematical grid pattern using squares or rectangles called "blocks." Addresses are numbered along the streets that form the edges of the blocks. Addresses with odd numbers tend to be found on one side of the street, even numbers on the other side. Some cities use a compasslike address system, such as North 3700, West 26900. Intersections are described by the names of the intersecting streets, such as "First and Center streets."

Big cities often use names, such as Broadway or Capitol Avenue, for their primary street names and numbers for secondary streets. Street names tend to go in connected groups in large cities, either numbered in order, such as First Street, Second Street, Third Street, or 210th Street, 210th Place, 210th Way, 211th Street, or alphabetically, A Street, B Street, C Street. State names such as Alabama Street, Carolina Street, or Delaware Street may be used or even the names of presidents of the United States in consecutive order, with Washington Street as the first street of the group. Some small towns use names of trees as street names, such as Oak Street and Maple Street. (Naming a street "Main Street" or with the name of a tree in television shows is intended to indicate a small town; a number for a street name indicates a big city.)

In large cities, walking distance is measured in "blocks." You can usually walk two or three blocks in five minutes. Ten blocks could take a half hour. Ten blocks to the mile and twenty blocks to the mile are two standard distance measures, determined by the size of a block in that city. Since a kilometer is equal to 0.6 mile, a mile should be considered the equivalent of 2 kilometers.

To get to know your city better, get a map of the public transportation system and match the transit routes on it with your map of the city. If there is a fixed rail system, either above ground or below ground, such as a trolley, light rail, or subway (underground rail system), study the maps until you can determine where and how to change trains, which stop will be closest to your destination, and which end of the station will help you avoid walking extra blocks. If there are buses, ask the people who work with the system where you can get a description of the routes and a timetable. The more information you have, the more comfortable you will feel.

TRANSPORTATION

As you begin exploring, you will notice there is a social hierarchy to methods of travel in the U.S.A. Public transportation and long-distance bus lines are the least favored; trains are one step above. Cars and airplanes are the highest on the hierarchy, just as in other countries.

Bicycles

For cheap independent transportation, consider getting a bicycle. If you are at a university, the best place to look for one, other than in the Yellow Pages of the telephone book under "Bicycles-Dealers" or in the daily newspaper classified advertising section, is on the walls of supermarkets or grocery stores near the university. The market for used bikes is always brisk near a college or university.

Riding a bicycle does not exempt you from traffic rules. Most states require that bicycles be registered with a police station or fire department, in case of loss or accident, and that they be equipped with reflectors. Most cities do not allow bicycles to be ridden after dark without a lamp attached to the front handlebars. It is the responsibility of the owner—not the seller of the bicycle—to comply with these regulations.

The decision to purchase a bike involves asking yourself a few questions: How often will it be used? Are there some months of the year in which I cannot use it? If so, where will I store it? A bicycle must be locked whenever you are not riding it, so that it will not be stolen; purchase a bicycle chain and padlock. A bicycle bag and basket are handy accessories to carry things, but you would be wise to resist any sales pressure to "trade up" to a bigger, fancier bike or bigger, fancier accessories at this stage.

Driving a Car

Some newcomers have false confidence about driving a car that comes from having an international driver's license—valid for a year from your date of arrival in the United States. The Appendix provides a list of countries that have reciprocal agreements with the United States to accept international driver's licenses. You must obtain the international driver's license together with an English translation of it, if necessary, in your country of origin.

If you come from a country where everyone drives on the left side of the road, it can take a while to get used to the American way of driving on the right side. We recommend driving lessons to get used to American road conditions; you may need just one or two. Driving schools charge by the hour, and you can use their cars to learn. Then you can get an American license or use your international license with safety. Driver's licenses are issued by your state's Department of Motor Vehicles. A license obtained in one state is valid for driving in all other states.

All states have both a written test and a driving test that you will need to pass to get a driver's license for that state. The minimum age to obtain a driver's license not requiring adult supervision varies from 15 in Mississippi to 21 in Georgia and Colorado.

Getting Around

The nonprofit American Automobile Association (AAA) publishes a useful guide called *Digest of Motor Laws*, describing the motor laws for all kinds of vehicles in every state in the United States. To request a copy, contact the Traffic Safety and Engineering Department, American Automobile Association, 1000 AAA Drive, Heathrow, FL 32746-5063.

Americans often think nothing of traveling to the next town to meet people for dinner or for a mini-vacation. Many people who live in cities with good public transportation and scarce parking like New York and San Francisco decide not to own a car and instead rent one on weekends if they need to travel outside the city. If a friend rents a car that you intend to drive as well, be sure to have your name listed on the rental agreement as an additional driver. That way, if you have an accident, you will be deemed an authorized driver and covered by any insurance that might apply. You can rent a car if you have a driver's license (international or American) and a well-known credit card (for instance, Visa or Master-Card) in just about any city in America.

American laws on driving while intoxicated are some of the strictest in the world. Most states have laws that

From a car window (Photo by Shauna Singh Baldwin)

assume your consent to a chemical test for drugs and alcohol is implied by your being on the road. If you are found to be intoxicated, in some states, your license can be suspended on the spot; in others, punishments can vary from car confiscation to imprisonment. Speed limits on four-lane highways are now 55 miles per hour in populated areas and 65 miles per hour in sparsely populated areas. In most states, if you are caught speeding three times, you can lose your license. There are fines for littering highways in every state.

Local Buses
There are small buses that take people to and from downtown or outlying hotels and the airport; these are usually referred to as "airport limousines." Larger buses are considered mass transit and are usually the cheapest form of public transportation. You are expected to have the exact fare for your ride on a bus. You usually pay as you enter for a single ride; a "pass" will let you ride all you want for a short period of time, perhaps a week. "Transfers" are pieces of paper you can use instead of paying extra fare if you need to take more than one bus to reach your destination. Transfers are valid for only a short time—as little as one hour, as much as four hours, or occasionally the whole day. You can ask the bus driver for the transfer as you pay your fare. You can also ask the bus driver to let you know when you have arrived at your transfer point or your final destination.

Long-Distance Bus Lines
All long-distance bus companies (Greyhound is the best known) are privately owned, rather than tax supported. Bus companies do not take reservations in larger cities; you simply have to be in the terminal at the time the bus is scheduled to leave; if there are more people who wish to travel than one bus can hold, the company will usually add a second bus to avoid losing customers. In smaller towns, you can sometimes make a reservation and buy your ticket on the bus. Buses make stops in many towns, so before the bus leaves the terminal, ask the driver if you are on the right bus. You are not expected to tip the bus driver for any services provided.

Riding the bus (Photo by Shauna Singh Baldwin)

Greyhound will transport unaccompanied baggage; the service is known as Greyhound Package Express (GPX). This is an excellent means of transporting some personal effects across the country without using a professional moving company. Greyhound offers "door-to-door" (more expensive) and "counter-to-counter" (less expensive) service. You can call Greyhound in your city for a price quotation based on current rates. They will need to know the zip code of your destination to give you pricing and the number of boxes so as to calculate a multiple-shipment discount. Package all your items carefully, and either take them to the bus company baggage counter or call and request door-to-door pickup of your boxes.

Greyhound offers 7-day, 15-day, and 30-day Ameripass tickets that allow unlimited travel anywhere in the country on their buses. These are available from any Greyhound station and may be a bargain compared to individual fares.

You will not need to take food with you for a trip, unless you have a dietary restriction. Most bus terminals sell food and even have restaurants. Eating on a bus is allowed; so is drinking nonalcoholic beverages. Long-distance buses have rest rooms on board, but for cleanliness, we recommend using the terminal rest room if possible. Bus companies in the United States have to meet National Transportation Safety Board standards; you will find buses quite comfortable for long journeys.

Trains

The only long-distance passenger train company is called Amtrak, which is a government-owned enterprise. Trains are used primarily for industrial transport today. It may come as a surprise to many newcomers that there are many Americans who have never traveled by train.

Passenger trains in America are quite clean, safe, and spacious. On overnight journeys, sleeping cars and dining cars can make the journey more comfortable. Some of the luxury cabins for overnight travel can increase the cost of your journey until it is about the same as airfare, but train travel has a romance that is quite enticing. Many newcomers tell us the America of Hollywood's western movies and Norman Rockwell pictures can be found while traveling by rail.

You can "check" your bags onto a special luggage car on most trains, but commuter trains that travel short distances from the suburbs to the city often do not have luggage cars and may assess a fine if you carry on suitcases or other large items. Buy a sturdy travel cart with wheels for all long-distance travel by rail. Amtrak's Red Cap porters are available only in larger cities, and they expect to be tipped generously.

Amtrak offers an "All Aboard America" fare, similar to Europe's Eurorail pass. These fares are based on 45 days of travel through the eastern, mid-America, or western regions of the country but necessitate a planned itinerary. Fare prices drop during the "value season" of January through May. Within the United States, you can call 1-800-USA-RAIL (1-800-872-7245) for the latest information and rates.

Airplanes

Unlike many countries, the United States does not have a national airline, nor are any of the airline companies owned or operated by the government. Airports, however, are owned by local governments and are therefore tax supported. This may explain why airline companies in the United States go in and out of business on a frequent basis, while airports are a little more stable.

You can buy tickets directly from an airline or through a travel agent. The travel agent has no power, in America, to get you a better seat, to change a waitlisted reservation to a confirmed one, or to waive any airline penalties. However, a travel agent—particularly one who serves a specific ethnic group—can get you a cheaper international fare if he or she buys airplane seats in large enough quantities from one airline. The travel agent gets a commission from the airline and should not mark up anything sold to you.

All airlines have baggage restrictions: usually one carryon bag that can fit beneath your seat and up to two suitcases to be checked in. For short distances, commuter planes are likely to have more restrictions. It is sometimes a long walk between gates, so either carry your own baggage cart if you are flying into any major city or keep your carryon baggage to a minimum. Some airports have baggage carts that you can rent in the baggage claim area, and many have porters. But as with most things in America, do-it-yourself is cheaper.

Whatever the size of the plane or the airport, some rules are universal. Do not carry weapons in your luggage, particularly in carryon luggage. This includes ceremonial swords, knives, plastic toy pistols, and hunting equipment. If you have to transport these items, call the airline and ask how you should do this. All airports have security scanning equipment for baggage. (A few places still have outmoded equipment that could damage rolls of film or computer diskettes that are passed through it.) Both carryon and checked-in baggage is scanned. Many airports require people carrying personal computers to supply power for them at the security checkpoints, so you should not pack the power cord or battery pack in your checked-in luggage. Do not make jokes about hijacking, bombing, or otherwise harming the flight; you can be fined for such behavior.

All the larger airlines have frequent flyer programs through which people can get free tickets, upgrades, or gifts for flying a large number of miles on the same airline. Foreign students traveling to and from the home country can often get credit for international travel—lots of air mileage! We recommend signing up for these, unless there is a fee associated with signing up. Refuse anyone's offer to sell you a frequent flyer ticket; if an airline discovers that you have purchased such a ticket, your ticket can be confiscated and any remaining travel on it will be at your own expense.

There is no charge for airport rest rooms in the United States, unlike some in Europe. Some airports have pay lockers for small bags, but they do not have Left Luggage facilities such as you find in major tourist cities of Europe. Special rest lounges in major airports are open to travel club members and offer business facilities and even meeting rooms. Most airports have automated teller machines and traveler's check dispensing machines, but these are only usable after you have established a banking relationship somewhere in the country. Pay phones can be found all over U.S. airports. Every airport has a Traveler's Aid desk or official responsible for providing information about a city to newcomers.

Only major airports have currency exchange counters, so if you fly directly into a smaller American city from Canada or Mexico, for example, try to bring enough U.S. dollars to last you a couple of days until you can find a local bank. U.S. airlines will not accept even Mexican or Canadian money for on-board duty-free purchases or earphone rentals for on-board movies. (If your U.S. visa was a single-entry visa, and you wish to return to the United States from Canada or Mexico, be sure to obtain permission for another entry prior to departure. Remember not to think of travel to Canada or Mexico as travel within the borders of the United States; your country may have different treaty arrangements with those countries.)

If you call 24 hours prior to departure, you can ask for any of the following special meals on a U.S. airline: kosher, fruit plate, vegetarian, low calorie, low

Getting Around

cholesterol, or diabetic. If you are allergic to any foods, you should specify foods to be excluded when requesting special meals.

If you plan to travel outside the United States temporarily, research the specific requirements of the U.S. Immigration and Naturalization Service for reentry. It is important to remember that you should not rely on the airline to provide this information or to obtain any necessary permissions and visas for you. The airline simply sells you a ticket; it is your responsibility to obtain permission to reenter the United States. For instance, customs and visa restrictions for Canadians and Mexicans entering from overseas are very different from those applied to Canadians and Mexicans entering over their respective borders. Canadians entering the United States from overseas for an extended stay require visas, for example.

Transporting illegal drugs (even prescription drugs not approved by the U.S. Food and Drug Administration; for example, RU486 pills) can be grounds for arrest, criminal charges, and even deportation.

Be courteous, and remember to treat members of the crew as your equals, not as your servants. Look out of the window as you fly. This is a beautiful country. Talk to people you meet in flight and to the crew. Americans tell perfect strangers things you may consider intimate details; they will talk about their sex lives, but do not ask them about their income or discuss America's role in global politics.

5 Housing

Land and all types of buildings are called "real estate" in the United States. Housing availability, in general, is greater than almost anywhere else in the world; however, finding housing that fits your needs and resources is easier in smaller towns than in larger cities. Government housing is only available for welfare recipients and certain groups of disabled people.

Most newcomers rely on friends for shelter for the first few days, but there is a limit to how long one can impose on the good nature, time, and resources of compatriots from the old country or new acquaintances here in America. Two weeks stay with friends at first arrival is normal for most newcomers, about a month if staying with family. Any longer can strain a relationship so it is best not to test it.

If you do not plan to stay with friends or family when you first arrive, you will need a hotel as soon as the Immigration and Naturalization Service officer has put the final stamp of entry approval in your passport. Most people begin by making arrangements for temporary housing until they have a better idea of what might suit them. One of the reasons university housing coordinators do not make arrangements for permanent housing for foreign students before they arrive is because they do not wish to be responsible for leases that become disputed because the newcomers do not like the premises.

HOTELS OR MOTELS

A very short-term housing option, a hotel or motel room near the airport, on a truck route, or near a bus station, is often the least expensive alternative for a first night. This sort of hotel is particularly useful if you arrive after dark. Most major airports have prominent hotel advertisements; many have a direct phone to the hotel attached to an information panel, so that you can call the hotel to request a "courtesy" bus to take you there. If you do not see any advertisements for hotels in your price range, find the nearest public pay phone and look up "Hotels" in the Yellow Pages telephone directory. Try to choose a hotel that offers a shuttle bus or limousine to take you into the city, where you can find more permanent shelter. If you expect to make overseas calls, ask if the hotel allows this from the rooms and how much extra they will charge.

The word "motel" is a contraction of "motor hotel," which expresses the expectation that guests will arrive in some form of personal motorized transport—cars or trucks. The clientele consists of vacationers, salespeople, truckers, and business travelers who do not want to pay city hotel prices. Downtown motels can be quite luxurious and cost just as much as any prestigious hotel.

It is quite acceptable to ask the desk clerk to show you the room before you accept it and "check in." The common practice in hotels and motels is to expect you to guarantee the funds for your stay by use of a credit card. If you have a credit card issued overseas that the hotel can and will accept, you should have no trouble. If you have no credit card, international traveler's checks and cash are necessary. Money can be exchanged during the daytime at most large airport banks or hotels for a fee based on the current exchange rates.

American hotels and motels always provide towels and soap when you rent a room. The higher the rate per night, the more toiletries they will probably place in the bathroom. While it is acceptable to take unused hotel soaps, shampoo bottles, and shower caps, taking a hotel's towels or ashtrays is a legally punishable offense.

If you find you do not have enough money to pay the invoice at the end of your stay, the management will examine your reasons for not having the money. What they will be looking for is a question of intent. If you come in knowing you do not have the funds to pay, or try to slip away without paying, you can be arrested; if you reach in your pocket and your wallet is gone, it becomes an issue of credit. If this last situation occurs, explain to the management what has happened, leave something of value as "collateral," and go find other sources of money. If you do not have the funds, you can ask your sponsor to assist you temporarily. Other resources include voluntary agencies, ethnic organizations, and international institutes.

HOSTELS

Youth hostels in the United States tend to be wilderness-oriented places to stay rather than cheap accommodations for young people, as is the case in other countries. If you would like your first housing in the United States to be at a youth hostel, it would be wise to check with the hosteling organization in your home country for more information about American hosteling before you leave home.

DORMITORIES AND RESIDENCE HALLS

Dormitories and residence halls offer students inexpensive rooms with shared dining and bath facilities. An example of a residence hall that can be found in most cities is the YMCA or YWCA. The letters stand for Young Men's (or Women's) Christian Association, but you don't have to be Christian to rent a room there. Most "Y"s have swimming pools and workout rooms. To find other places that offer transitional housing, refer to your city's Yellow Pages under "Hot Lines and Help Lines" or "Hotels," or the local newspaper in the classified advertising section under "Furnished Rooms" or "Furnished Accommodations."

There are some great advantages to living in a "dorm" or a residence hall. Besides the fact that there is a shared dining hall and the rooms are furnished, the residence halls are good places to watch how people react to one another and to you, to make friends, and to discover how diverse and individual Americans are.

You cannot legally be refused housing at a residence hall or dorm because of your race, color, or religion. The reality is that the message will never be stated bluntly if someone really does not wish to give you shelter; you might be politely told that the residence hall is "full."

If this happens to you and you can prove that the residence hall was not full and you were illegally denied

Undergraduates in a university dormitory (Photo courtesy of Marquette University)

housing, you can report it to the proper authorities and sue for damages in court at a later time. If all you really want is to find a place to stay, contact your sponsor, another newcomer, a voluntary agency, or a university housing office for a list of places that rent to students.

Once in a dorm or residence hall, you may find you have a greater tolerance for lack of privacy than many Americans. You would do well to be sensitive to tensions caused by what is perceived in America as "crowding." Do not:
- slip messages under a neighbor's door. Drop them off at the message center of the building.
- play loud music in your room.
- attempt to cook in a room where it is not allowed.
- make long or loud telephone calls when your neighbors may be waiting to use a shared phone.
- smoke in bed.

And be sure to:
- call before visiting a neighbor's room, if possible.
- always knock before entering a neighbor's room and wait for permission to enter.

SHARED ACCOMMODATIONS

One of the best ways to reduce living expenses is to share your living quarters with another person or to rent a room in a private home. To find someone who wishes to share accommodations, look at the free advertisement boards at most grocery stores near universities or in the local newspaper. The ads may say "Wanted—Roommate" or may be listed along with others in the section for furnished accommodations. You can assume that either sex is acceptable if the gender of the roommate desired is not specified. Private homes large enough to have a spare room are usually located in the "suburbs," away from the center of the city, and are therefore likely to be cheaper than a shared city apartment. Shared accommodations rarely offer you a private bathroom. Call the advertiser and ask to see the living quarters.

Assuming you like the place and the price is right, you and your landlord or prospective roommate have to decide whether you can live with one another. Remember that the person who has advertised can refuse you accommodation even if you can prove that you have the money to pay for your rent; both of you need to establish a level of trust to be able to live together. You must be assured that you will be treated with consideration as well.

It may seem rude to ask a stranger personal questions about his or her habits as soon as you meet, but it is important not to be surprised later. Here is a list of things to discuss with a prospective roommate. You will probably have many more questions of your own, but this is a start:

- When is your share of the rent due? What form of receipt for payment will your roommate or landlord give you to prove you have paid your rent?
- What are the additional expenses? Heat? Electricity? Water? When are these due, and approximately how much money will you have to pay per week or month as your contribution?
- Who does the furniture belong to? If it belongs to the advertiser, are there any items you would not be welcome to use?
- Can you use the kitchen? When? Can you keep food

in your room? In the landlord's refrigerator? Does your landlord include "board," or meal costs, with your rent and expect you to eat meals with the family and other boarders? Or are you expected to cook your own food and eat separately? Is meal preparation taken in turns? If you use the kitchen to cook your own food, must you have your own dishes? Has your roommate or landlord experienced your home country's cooking? What opinion has been formed of its smell?

- Is there a garage? Does your prospective landlord or roommate have a car? Is street parking allowed in the area close to the apartment? (You should ask this even if you do not have a car at present, as you may acquire one later.)
- How late is it acceptable to use the main entrance to the home? Who, besides yourself, will have a key? Is there a private entrance?
- How many rooms in the house are rented to other people? Would it be possible to meet the other tenants?
- Are there additional storage facilities in the apartment or home that you can use? Ask to see them.
- Does your roommate or landlord have children who live at home? How old are they? Ask to meet them, particularly if you plan to wear non-Western dress when at home.
- Does the homeowner or your prospective roommate smoke? If not, would he or she mind if you do? (You should discuss whether it would bother either party if someone—even a guest—were to smoke on the premises.)
- How much and in what ways do you and your prospective roommate or landlord like to entertain guests? How often will you or your roommate come home late at night?
- Does your roommate or landlord have any pets? If so, what are they? (Ask to meet them.) Are pets allowed on the furniture? Are they allowed to eat off crockery or only from their own bowls? Where do they sleep?
- Can you invite a guest to share your room for the night? (The answer is usually yes if it is a relative but

no if it is a romantic interest.)
- What are the rules about using the telephone? Would your roommate understand if you receive calls from overseas in the middle of the night? Can you have a telephone in your own room? (This is often the best solution; telephones are easily installed by the telephone company.)
- How often will either of you have visitors to stay? How many visitors does each person consider normal? Where will they sleep? How long would the other person feel comfortable hosting your live-in guests?

The person who has leased the apartment and accepted a roommate is the one who sets the rules of the house and enforces them; the other person has the right to leave in cases of extreme disagreement. If both people sign the lease with the landlord, both are liable for the rent, and house rules become a matter of equal negotiation. If one person decides to move out before the other, the person who moves should find someone else to move in or give enough notice so that the person who remains can find someone to "sublease" the apartment. This way, the person who remains does not become liable for the whole rent. The landlord is under no obligation to seek out the person who has left to collect that portion of the rent.

Two issues that can cause friction even between people of the same culture are money and privacy. It is important to realize that your agreement to pay your share of the rent has to be discharged in money. As an immigrant, your assets are often in kind, not cash, but this does not help your roommate pay the landlord or the landlord pay his or her property taxes. Another common misconception held by newcomers with socialist backgrounds is that the one with greater assets at the time should pay what is due or be willing to extend credit until the other has enough money to pay. This expectation will rarely be met in the United States.

It is, however, common practice to agree to pay only that portion of the telephone bill for which you are responsible. We recommend that roommates should buy their own laundry detergent, toilet articles, food, and expensive or alcoholic beverages. As you get to know one another, you may wish to share.

It will take a while to judge the extent of one another's need for privacy. A rule of thumb we recommend is to ask if your roommate or landlord comes from a large family; if so, he or she is likely to be used to less privacy than a person who comes from a small family. You can also ask where your roommate comes from, the size of the town or city, for example. The smaller the population in the town or city, the more solitude and privacy the person is likely to be used to. The best way to treat a roommate is with consideration, and you will then be entitled to expect the same. Treat your landlord's property with as much care as you would treat your own and replace any items you use in the same condition as you found them.

Here is a short list of unpardonables that you should be aware of:

- leaving hair in the tub or shower or sink after use.
- rearranging your roommate's furniture or rearranging furniture in your landlord's portion of the house.
- inviting a person of the opposite sex over to stay the night without permission.
- trying to convert your roommate or landlord to your religion or denomination.
- using your roommate's or landlord's car without permission.
- not paying your share of the rent, electricity, heat, or telephone bill on time.

APARTMENT HOTELS

Apartment hotels are housing alternatives that cater to single people or couples without children. You can find these advertised under "Hotels" in the Yellow Pages; many also advertise in the classified section of the newspaper under "Furnished Apartments." Some apartments are just large bedrooms with sitting areas. This is called a "studio" apartment. Apartment hotels generally have a message center and provide soap and towels and laundry facilities and may have a small restaurant. Maid service is usually offered if you agree to pay extra for it.

YOUR OWN APARTMENT

Renting an apartment of one's own is the first step to independence for most American young people—a step that their parents often encourage so that their children will be self-reliant. (Americans often forget this is a luxury possible because of low population density.) To an American, a 30-year-old building is old; a 100-year-old building is *really* old. Old apartment buildings will not usually have central air-conditioning, and some have no elevators, but many have character and low rents that compensate.

American landlords are somewhat like the immigration authorities. When you want to come in, they can be nasty and suspicious, but once you are in, you become part of the group to be protected. Foreigners are given no special preference in housing (or anything else) as they are in some countries. As a last resort, a classified advertisement in the local newspapers stating your housing needs and your origin can be effective. It may also reduce your chances of unpleasant encounters since only open-minded owners who really like the idea of cultural exchange will be likely to respond.

Rental properties usually include major appliances. In apartments, this means a stove, a refrigerator, and sometimes a dishwasher. In rental homes, this means a stove, a refrigerator, and sometimes a dishwasher, a washer, and a dryer. Kitchens in old apartments tend to be small and enclosed; a kitchen open to view from the living room or dining room is the 1990s standard.

Only expensive apartments have a bathroom for every bedroom. Every apartment can be expected to have one "full" bath. A full bath contains sink, toilet, and bathtub or shower; a "half bath" contains a toilet and sink only. Sometimes bathrooms are situated uncomfortably close to the kitchen in the opinion of newcomers from cultures with strong contamination beliefs. If you are concerned about this layout, you will find it takes a little longer to find accommodations.

If you plan to have parents or in-laws staying with you for extended periods, you might consider looking for a "duplex" (a house with two units) or a "townhouse," a unit with rooms on several levels. Some real estate "developers" (people who build properties and sell them to others) are beginning to build houses with "mother-in-law" sections to accommodate the customs of some Asian-Americans on the West Coast, but these are expensive. Some large developments, called "condominiums," have apartments that are owned individually, with the outside land and halls held by the condominium association. Buying two condominium apartments next to one another can also be a solution to the need for "mother-in-law" accommodations.

Try not to enter into long leases (leases over 2 months in the case of an apartment and over 1 year in the case of a house) until you are familiar with your surroundings. While a lease ensures that a landlord may not raise the rent for that period, it also makes your situation less flexible than you might wish if you are still in a period of evaluation and adjustment. Classified advertisements in the real estate section of the newspaper can help you find a cheap, clean apartment or house for rent in good condition not too far from the location of your expected activities.

Decide on your budget. The rule of thumb in the United States is to spend about 25 percent of one's yearly income on shelter. If this seems excessive, consider bartering work for shelter. (For instance, look for work as a caretaker manager or as "live-in" help, which will include housing.)

We can find no uniformity in the use of terms in housing advertisements except for the use of LR, DR, and BR as abbreviations for living room (drawing room), dining room, and bedroom (sleeping room), respectively. While you can assume that a "flat" is the second floor of a house, an "apartment" is part of a building in which there are other apartments, and a "studio" means that the living room converts to the sleeping quarters at night, there is no substitute for seeing the place yourself.

Legally, no one is allowed to deny housing to anyone because of race, religion, or national origin. But if you find yourself being told "We just rented it" a little too often for your liking, find yourself a rental agent who will be more accepted in the neighborhood to make inquiries on your behalf. Rental agents are usually paid by the owner of the rental property.

When the landlord shows you around the apartment, be sure to ask if the furniture you see will stay. When was the last time an exterminator was called in to get rid of bugs? Where should you dispose of trash, and how often is it picked up? Are there laundry facilities? How much do they cost? Are guests allowed for extended stays? Are pets or children allowed? When will the current tenant move out? Will the landlord have the apartment cleaned and/or repainted before you move in? (If you are willing to do the work, landlords will sometimes provide the paint.) When can you move in? While the landlord does not have to tell you, you can ask discreetly about who lives next door.

If the living quarters are old or something in the apartment is broken, you can try asking for a reduction in rent. Alternatively, ask when the manager plans to make repairs. In some cities, where competition for tenants is high, you can refuse to move in until repairs are complete, but do not try this in a larger city.

Introduce or talk about your spouse, children, and anyone else who will be living with you or visiting for extended periods as a security precaution and to prevent a request for additional rent for additional occupants.

To assess the neighborhood, ask: What is the best way to get to your most frequent activity from the apartment? Does the route you will travel seem safe? Where is the closest grocery store? Where is the closest convenience store? Is there a dry cleaner or laundromat nearby?

If you like the housing, the next step is to obtain and read a written lease; verbal leases are assumed to be month-to-month only. Read the agreement carefully before you sign; if necessary, ask a friend, university professor, or real estate broker to look it over. If you plan to share expenses, have the other(s) sign the lease as well. If you have pets or children, make sure the lease states that it is all right for them to be present in the building.

When you give the landlord the signed lease, keep a

copy for yourself. Along with the signed lease, you will be expected to pay the landlord the first month's rent in advance plus the security deposit.

If the apartment is in a tall building and you have heavy or bulky items to be moved, ask the manager (usually the person you will deal with) to "reserve an elevator" (lift) on the day you plan to move in. Moving day is always hectic even if you have only your clothing to move. Inspect the apartment before you bring in your possessions, to ensure that the owner repaired everything agreed upon. If the apartment does not look as you expected, call the manager or owner and discuss it. Do not move in if a necessary appliance or fixture is not functioning. Once you have settled all your possessions, put up some pictures of home and family as decoration and as anchor for yourself and go to the grocery store and buy some food to test your culinary skills and your new oven or order pizza. It will do wonders for your morale.

FURNISHING YOUR NEW HOME

If you are renting a furnished apartment, your basic furniture will be supplied by the landlord; you can add any of your own possessions as you acquire them. Your things will move with you when you leave the apartment, but the landlord's possessions remain.

If you are renting an unfurnished apartment in this land of highly mobile people, you can rent everything you need. You can rent a telephone from the telephone company. You can rent furniture. (Check for cleanliness, however.) Furniture rental store "rent-to-own" plans include interest and should be compared with new furniture "layaway plans" offered by department stores. You can rent TVs, VCRs, sofas, dinettes, beds—anything to furnish your place. Some of these rental companies have executive (fancy) furniture, and others have functional but plain furniture. It is an excellent way to ensure your own mobility. When you want to move, you simply call the rental company. They will pick up the furniture and take it away.

If you decide to collect some possessions, your options

are limited only by the size of your wallet. You can usually find excellent bargains without having to travel far out of your neighborhood. The closest you can come in America to a bazaar bargaining experience would be at a "rummage" (jumble) or "garage" sale. These are occasional one- or two-day sales at which people use their garages, yards, and driveways as showrooms for all sorts of things they are tired of or need to throw away. These sales are advertised in the local newspaper on weekends, as are "estate" sales, which are sales of personal possessions occurring after someone dies.

You are likely to have the most trouble finding "window treatments"—drapes or curtains. Try to rent or buy a place that has existing drapes; anything custom made in the United States is likely to be expensive. If you are handy with a needle, rummage sale drapes can sometimes be cut to fit.

Other sources of cheap furnishings are used furniture stores and nonprofit stores run by Goodwill or the Salvation Army. (Goodwill and the Salvation Army are highly respected nonprofit organizations helping the poor. In addition, the Salvation Army is a Christian denomination.) Sometimes used furniture may have the potential to appreciate in value as an "antique." Keep this in mind as you shop.

HOUSING FOR COUPLES WITH CHILDREN

Temporary housing in the form of a furnished apartment that can be rented by the day or week can often be obtained for a family by checking with the local office for tourists or the bulletin boards at a college or university in the area. University housing offices sometimes have a list of off-campus rentals for incoming graduate students and faculty; families who need such accommodations only briefly may be able to persuade a landlord to let them use the premises until a more permanent tenant arrives.

It is illegal to discriminate against families with children when renting or selling a house or apartment, unless it is in a building with less than four rental units with an owner in residence or any complex in which all residents are 62 years of age or older.

DISPUTES AND RIGHTS

If you wish to move, you usually need to give the property owner written notice one month in advance for a month-to-month lease to make sure you get your security deposit back. On longer-term leases, there is usually a provision set by the landlord.

A landlord cannot legally lock you out of your apartment to evict you if your rent is overdue. If you do not have a written lease and your rent is overdue, your landlord must give you a "5-day quit" or "pay rent notice." After you get this notice, you must pay your rent or vacate in five days. Eviction is possible only if the owner obtains a court order. If you receive a "summons," a legal document threatening a lawsuit for nonpayment of rent, you should call an attorney. If you cannot afford an attorney in private practice, state attorneys at your local county courthouse, called "public defenders," can assist you.

Property owners are allowed to set the amount of rent in most areas of the country. They are also allowed to set rules and regulations for the tenant; for example, they have the right to refuse to rent to families with pets. The owner may inspect the premises at reasonable times, giving the tenant reasonable notice in advance. An owner may ask you to vacate the premises with one month's notice if you do not have a lease. An owner has the right to sell the rental building or unit if the building becomes a condominium. If your unit is sold and you have no clause to the contrary, your lease continues until its expiration date.

You can report violations of state rental laws by a landlord to your state Department of Justice, Office of Consumer Protection, or the equivalent. However, they can do little to help except to mediate between two opposing parties. A pattern of abuse is required before legal action can be taken.

Your home is your castle. Dare to express your personality, your style, your heritage and your taste. It is possible to do it here without spending a lot of money. And remember that you can always move.

6 Cooking at Home

Cooking at home is cheaper than eating out and in smaller towns and cities, may be the only way to partake of food from your home country. Most immigrant populations have managed to find substitutes for labor-intensive or hard-to-find food items from the old country. Libraries and bookstores are sure to have a cookbook written by one of your compatriots for an American kitchen; you will find many substitutes and even shortcuts that will allow you to maintain your old food habits to some extent. Even so, do not be afraid to try new food products—as long as you know what is in them.

Almost all food shopping in this country is done by "self-service"; everything is stored on shelves and you load up a shopping cart with all the items you wish to buy and take it to a cashier or clerk at the "checkout counter" so that you can pay for it. Many different types of stores sell food.

At the checkout counter (Photo by Shauna Singh Baldwin)

A farmer's market stand

Fresh seasonal fruits and vegetables (sometimes called "produce") are best at a local "farmers market." There you will find unpackaged cabbages, onions, potatoes, carrots, tomatoes, and peppers, which will be weighed and put in a bag, possibly by the person who picked them that morning. Ask your neighbors where they are.

"Convenience" stores are located in high-traffic areas. They offer convenience at higher prices. "Gourmet" and "specialty" stores are often about the same size as convenience stores but a lot more attractive and expensive. These may be stores that only stock, say, coffee or tea, the ingredients for the cuisine of a particular country, or general gourmet items.

Most American families shop once or twice a week at a "grocery store" or "supermarket," sometimes traveling a distance to find the lowest prices and the largest selection. Many American families own large refrigerators and freezers to keep on hand food that was purchased when the price was low.

At the supermarket (Photo by Shauna Singh Baldwin)

The first time you visit a "warehouse" supermarket, you may be overwhelmed by the number of items displayed and the not-so-subtle invitation to spend money. These are larger supermarkets that use their shelving as storage. While you may have a longer walk down their aisles, their prices are often lower than a regular supermarket can offer.

Department stores sometimes sell food, too. Think of their food department as a grocery store connected to other stores. Department stores that have food departments tend to stock only higher priced or gourmet items. If you cannot find an item that was considered a staple part of your diet in the old country—candied ginger or phyllo dough or kimchee or mangoes—try the food department of a department store or a gourmet shop. Spices are stocked in every grocery store but are often stale because American cooking does not often call for more than salt and pepper (although we should point out that people in larger cities with more diverse populations and greater health consciousness are more willing to experiment in a culinary sense). It is best to search for a specialty food store from your area of the world;

America has a multitude of these. If there is none in your town or city, ask another newcomer, even one from a neighboring country of origin. This information is usually passed by word of mouth.

Supermarkets sell American specialty foods, such as the all-American "donut" (also "doughnut") and fresh bread at the bakery "counter." They also are likely to have a delicatessen counter, perhaps even a kosher deli. This is an area where sandwich meats, cheese, prepared salads, and sometimes sandwiches are sold. Remember to use U.S. Customary weights (thinking in Imperial weights will do just as well); if necessary, refer to the chart provided in the Appendix. The clerk will measure and package the items you desire and mark the price on them. You may be asked to pay for these items right away or with the rest of your groceries at the regular store checkout counter.

Larger supermarkets are likely to have a film department, a flower shop, a video rental counter, a pharmacy ("chemist"), and even a small bank. Many supermarkets have kosher food sections. Do not hesitate to use the telephone to locate a store that fills your needs. To find a food store in your neighborhood, check the telephone directory, walk around the area, or ask your neighbors.

EQUIPPING YOUR KITCHEN

If you are renting a furnished apartment, your kitchen should come equipped with a stove and a refrigerator, kitchen utensils, a few dishes, and some pots and pans. If you are living in unfurnished accommodations, you will need to buy a few kitchen items so that you can cook most types of meals in an American kitchen.

There are lists in the Appendix that will help you equip your new kitchen quickly and cheaply. New items may be purchased at a Woolworth's, Woolco, Wal-Mart, K-mart, or equivalent, at some supermarkets at slightly higher prices, or at a department store. Used items may be purchased at a thrift store (Salvation Army store or others like it) or at a rummage sale or garage sale. Sometimes an older resident will give you unneeded equipment if asked.

BUYING FOOD

We recommend that you purchase only minimal supplies for your kitchen on your first trip to an American grocery store. (Our recommended minimal supplies list is in the Appendix.)

Newcomers to this country are often unused to the idea of self-service in a store. It can be quite overwhelming to see the number of items available, and one can get confused between what is *necessary* and what is *desirable*. Take a pen and paper with you and write down what you think you *need* from the items displayed with their prices. In fact, you will find it helpful to get in the habit of making a shopping list before shopping; this will help you budget both your time and your money more effectively. If you set an upper limit on the total amount you plan to spend, when an "impulse" item comes along (something you had not planned to buy that looks inviting), you know whether or not you can afford it.

After you have made your list, look in the newspaper for "coupons." These are pieces of paper that offer you a price reduction if you purchase a particular brand and present the coupon at the checkout counter. There are two kinds of coupons. One reflects the food manufacturer's attempt to create "brand awareness" and usually does not have an expiration date. Grocery stores and supermarkets try to create "store awareness" by offering coupons that encourage you to come into the store to buy certain staple items for a "limited time only." If you see a coupon that asks for your name and address for a "sweepstake," this is really a way for the store to add your name to its mailing list to send you advertisements in the mail. This information is what you exchange for the possibility of a "free TV." Nothing is free; but then, no one can or will force you to write down your name and address on the coupon, either.

Do not trust the pictures on food packaging. They reflect what the food company would like you to imagine. (To make the food in the photograph look better, they may have used "make-up," perhaps even waxing fruit to create a shine.)

The objective of the food manufacturer and distributor

Cooking at Home

is to preserve the food for "maximum shelf life" (length of time on the shelf) while taking up as little shelf space as possible. Usually, the higher the fat and preservative content, the lower the price of the product. The trouble is, some of the foods that are the worst offenders are considered delicacies in countries where processed food is a novelty. There is no harm in buying a few of these items—they are designed for convenience, after all—but do not lose sight of the fact that a balanced diet gives you the strength and energy you need.

In America, manufacturers have to disclose food contents on their packaging, so read the label; this is especially important if you are trying to maintain any dietary restrictions for medical or religious reasons. For example, baked beans have often been a source of much mental discomfort to people who do not eat meat or perhaps do not eat pork; some baked beans are canned in a sauce made with pork. If this is a problem for you, you should look for canned beans made "vegetarian" style, or "Boston" style (with brown sugar).

When you select new foods in the supermarket or grocery store, or even when you are making your list, try to choose items that are not only cheap but also nutritious. Nutritious items are those that are low in fat content and will give you a balanced complement of vitamins, protein, and minerals. Try to choose foods that are fresh and natural with as little preservative as possible. Trust the small letters and charts on the label. The ingredients printed on the label are listed in descending order of amount; the first one listed is the largest. Nutrition information is given per serving; check the size of the serving.

Grocery stores sell food for dogs and cats as well as food for human beings, so do not be confused by a label that says "dog food." It is not canned dog meat but food designed to keep pet dogs healthy. While it will not kill you to eat it, it is better to buy food that will keep *you* healthy. "Hot dogs," however, are sausages made from beef (cow), pork (pig), or turkey and designed for human consumption. (The hot dog is a traditional food at baseball games, spread with a bit of mustard and pickle relish or sauerkraut, placed in a a bun, and eaten as a sandwich while shouting your approval or disapproval of the play on the field.)

YOUR RELATIONSHIP WITH THE FOOD STORE

The food marketing industry in the United States is subject to many stringent regulations concerning health and truth in advertising. This makes it improbable that any item would be sold in reused packaging or adulterated. Adulteration of food would be considered against the objective of maintaining a good image with all consumers.

Before opening each item you brought home from the store, check for any evidence of tampering. Although store owners take care that no tampering occurs, it is impossible for them to check every single item in the store. If a box of cereal that you bought seems to have been opened, do not touch the contents. Tell the store about it so that they can check all the rest of the cereal boxes in the same lot. Besides getting a refund for the item, it may save someone else from any adulteration that might have been attempted.

Food manufacturers are anxious for the consumer—that is, you—to know their brand and its distinctive quality in contrast to all other brands of the same item. They may employ people to offer you free samples to taste in the store. It is not impolite to refuse anything offered.

Fresh fruit, meat, pastries, and take-out food are displayed on open shelves for your selection, but we must caution it is considered unmannerly to taste the fruit (grapes and cherries are a prime example) before you put it in your shopping cart. It can even be considered "shoplifting," that is, stealing. Be careful not to unwrap meat to test it for redness or smell it; any items you unpackage will be considered sold to you, since the assumption is that they cannot then be sold to anyone else. Some bakeries in grocery stores offer a plate with bite-size pieces of baked goods specifically for testing. These will usually be unpackaged or uncovered, but the best policy is to ask. When in doubt, assume that the item is *not* free, and then it will be a pleasant surprise if it is.

This may seem unjust to you if you are used to a different way, but remember that the store takes responsibility for freshness and what is called "fitness for use." If the store is well-managed, it will be willing to replace any item that turns out to be spoiled or tampered with in any way, as long as you keep your receipt and return it as soon as possible. In addition, if you find after returning home with your purchases that you have paid for an item that was left out of your shopping bag, you should call the store immediately, give them your name, and ask that they either refund the money to you when you next go to the store with your receipt or that they set the item aside for you to pick up the same day.

DISPOSING OF PACKAGING

When you unwrap your purchases at home, you will need to dispose of the packaging; there is always a lot of it. If your kitchen sink has a garbage disposal, be careful not to put any plastic wrap or styrofoam into it. (Garbage disposals are for small bones and soft *food* products only, not soft items in general.) Most apartment buildings have garbage incinerator chutes. Unsafe items in these chutes include glass (it breaks as it goes down the chute) and aerosol cans (they burst when heated). If you come from a culture where you have been used to saving and reusing packaging, we hope you will not forget this habit completely. It will save you money in the short run, as you will not have to buy garbage bags and food storage containers (until the packaging threatens to take over your home). In the long run, remembering this habit will make relearning it less painful, and you will be right in step with those Americans who are starting to "recycle" on a regular basis.

Many apartment buildings and complexes have a separate disposal location for newspapers, bottles, aluminum cans, and cloth items. If so, you will need to separate these items from other garbage so that they can be recycled. If there is no such area, some cities provide a monetary incentive to recycle cans and bottles if you take them to the collection center yourself.

APPLIANCES

Most kitchens come equipped with large appliances such as an electric or gas stove and a refrigerator. Some also include a microwave oven and a dishwasher. You may wish to purchase some small appliances such as a toaster or toaster-oven for bread and light baking, an automatic electric coffee maker, perhaps an electric mixer or small food processor, a clock-radio or small television set, and perhaps an automatic electric rice cooker.

The flame in a gas oven may not turn on when you set the temperature. Older gas ovens require a lit match to ignite the gas for cooking. Ask someone to show you the location of all pilot lights on your gas stove (top and oven) and tell you which need to be ignited manually.

Some newcomers are nervous about using a microwave oven or eating food prepared in a microwave oven.

An American kitchen

Cooking at Home

These ovens have been in use since the 1950s in this country with no ill effects and have freed people from hours of food preparation. Their main value lies in quickly heating foods; they are not good for cooking anything that needs to be browned.

If you plan to buy a microwave oven at a later date, it would be best to purchase what are called "microwave-safe" pots and pans. These are usually made of glass or ceramic. Certain plastic containers can also be used, but check before buying. Metal of any kind must *not* be used in a microwave oven. This applies to dishes with gold or silver rims as well as metal pans.

The larger the number of people you need to cook and wash up for in your kitchen, the sooner you will want to acquire a mechanical dishwasher. If you are buying a used dishwasher (look in the classified section of the newspaper,) try to be sure it is not over 10 years old. Dishwashers normally last about 10 to 15 years. Between the tenth year and the fifteenth year, it is better to throw them out than to repair them.

You can purchase a new dishwasher at a department store or a large specialty appliance center. Most dishwashers come with instructions and a minimum warranty period. If you resolve to make a habit of rinsing dishes in the sink before you put them in the dishwasher, you can do without an extended warranty despite store pressure to purchase one. Consumer products sold in the United States are generally of excellent quality and do not break down very often. You would probably come out ahead in the long term by calling a repair service if your appliance breaks.

Before you call a repair service for a dishwasher, however, be sure that you do not actually have a plumbing problem. The repair service will charge you for a visit, just for the time spent, even if it turns out there was nothing to be fixed.

Even if you have a dishwasher, there are many items that you will need to wash by hand; these include thin plastic, items with wooden parts or handles, fine glassware, silver, and any handpainted ceramics. A different dishwashing detergent is required for use with these machines than for hand washing, and most machines require a bottle of "rinsing-aid" solvent once a month to assist the washing process.

RECIPES

A newcomer to this country once remarked that every time she asked an American for a recipe, she was told the ingredients and then "put in a little bit of salt, a little bit of pepper, and put it in the oven!" Recipes, whether from the newspaper or from cookbooks, are easy to follow once you know what some of the terms mean. Consult the glossary in this book if you are unfamiliar with American cooking.

Some newcomers mention that it is often difficult to convert old country recipes for use in America because America uses a different system of weights and measures. A conversion table is provided in the Appendix. There are two kinds of "ounces" in the American measuring system: one is for things that can be poured, such as fluids or powders, measured at 8 ounces to the cup; the other is used for weight and measures 16 ounces to the pound. You can tell which kind of ounce is being used because pourable things are measured in fractions of cups, such as "one-quarter (¼) *cup*," while weighed items are quoted by the fraction of a pound, as "¼ *pound*." When you buy fruits or vegetables or prepared foods at the store, the measure is by weight. You will ask for "one-quarter of a pound" of something, such as prepared salad, and you will get 4 ounces by weight.

Just to confuse you even more, things like nuts are sold by weight but measured in cups when used in recipes. If the recipe calls for ¼ cup of chopped nuts, for example, you might buy a package of walnut nutmeats that weighs 2 ounces and measures, according to the package, ½ cup, or up to the 4-ounce line on a measuring cup. To get your ¼ cup of chopped nuts, you must take the nuts out of the package, chop them, then put the chopped nuts in a measuring cup up to the 2-ounce or ¼ cup line. That kind of "2 ounces" of chopped nuts, called ¼ cup of chopped nuts, will probably weigh about 1 ounce out of the 2 in the package, leaving you with 1

ounce of chopped nuts for other recipes.
Approximations:
- One-half liter of liquid or 225 grams of dry material will fill an 8-ounce measuring cup for cooking purposes.
- One liter of liquid, such as milk, is the practical equivalent of a quart of liquid; 5 deciliters is the practical equivalent of 1 pint or 8 ounces of liquid.
- A half-gallon of any liquid is about 2 liters.
- A pound of vegetables or meat (16 ounces) is about .45 kilograms or just under 500 grams in weight.
- 100 grams of dry food is just under ½ cup dry measure.
- "A pint's a pound the world around": 8 ounces of wet food that comes in cans or jars, such as jams or jellies, will weigh 1 pound or 16 ounces on a scale.

As you get more familiar with your kitchen and acquire more friends, you may want to entertain. There are many excellent recipes to enable you to do this on a low budget, and the public library is an excellent source of cookbooks. Larger newspapers and magazines carry recipes and shortcuts for entertaining, and there are even programs for a personal computer that will suggest recipes to fit the ingredients you have at hand. Cooking does not have to be a burden or restricted only to women. In America, men cook as well as women and enjoy doing so.

CLEANING UP

Dishwashing liquid is such a common part of American life that few bottles give instructions on use; most of them merely say that their product leaves your hands looking as good as before. Wearing rubber gloves while washing dishes gives your hands even more protection.

To wash your dishes with dishwashing liquid, first clear the leftover food off your dishes with a fork or knife, then run water over them to rinse away any particles that can be easily dislodged. Then fill up a dishpan in the kitchen sink or close the drain in the sink and fill it halfway with warm or even hot water, adding about 2 tablespoons of the liquid as the water fills the sink to make suds. Soak your dishes in the sudsy water for as long as you think it will take to dissolve the food particles left on the dishes. Some things like dried egg yolk or burned milk should be presoaked separately with a small amount of dishwashing liquid or cleanser directly on the spot before adding to the general wash. Then, using a reusable paper wipe, a sponge, or a kitchen dish brush, lift each dish from the sudsy water, scrub it all over, and place it aside, or, if you have a second sink, in the second sink.

When all the dishes are scrubbed clean, or doing each one in turn if you have room, turn on the tap and hold the sudsy dishes under the running water (as hot as you can stand it to kill germs) to get rid of the soap and suds. Set the rinsed dishes on the dish drainer to dry. If you need to use them before they are dry, wipe them off with a clean kitchen towel. Metal pots and pans made of aluminum or stainless steel without a nonstick coating are cleaned using hot water, cleanser or scouring powder with a plastic scrubber, or for very dirty pans, "steel wool" pads with soap already in them. Glass or ceramic and nonstick pans are cleaned using a plastic scrubber and dishwashing liquid. Enamel pots and pans may be merely washed with dishwashing liquid if not too dirty, or scrubbed after soaking to remove burned-on food.

We recommend that wooden boards used for cutting raw meat or chicken be cleaned thoroughly with hot water and cleanser after each use to prevent any harmful bacteria from getting into the crevices in the wood. Salmonella is a bacteria that lives in improperly processed raw meat. It can cause severe cramps and intestinal distress if it gets into your food.

In any culture, cooking at home is a wonderful way to keep a couple or larger family together. You can talk as you dine, and share chores associated with mealtime. But even if you are only setting up your kitchen for yourself, remember that cooking at home is an important part of looking after oneself. Take the time and care to make it an activity you can enjoy. A clean and neat kitchen is essential if your cooking is to look inviting for yourself and your family and friends.

7 Keeping Clean

Keeping yourself and your household clean is essential to feeling healthy or making your place look inviting, even if only for yourself.

PERSONAL CLEANLINESS

A list of items to minimally equip your bathroom is presented in the Appendix. Daily bathing for both men and women is encouraged in America. If you are uncomfortable with the idea of lying in a tub of water that becomes dirty, you may prefer to shower. If you come from a country where water is scarce, showering may take some getting used to. Both men and women are expected to smell clean and fresh at all times, and daily use of a deodorant and bath powder is essential.

Women in America are expected to shave under their arms and, especially when wearing a skirt and nylons, to shave their legs. Razor blades in this country are very sharp, so be careful the first time you use them to shave. There are few shaving creams or foams made especially for women, and those that do exist are usually expensive. American women use soap and water or men's shaving cream to avoid itchy legs. Depilatories, or chemical hair removers, are sold in drugstores but should be used with extreme care according to the directions and tested on a small area before using generally. Waxing of legs is possible at home but expensive if you want it done for you in a beauty salon. Shaving or waxing the "bikini line" is expected if you wear a swimsuit. For women, waxing the upper lip is becoming more common, especially since there are now products available in drugstores to do it yourself at home. Products for bleaching facial hair are available but are not considered essential.

Female newcomers are often surprised by the unabashed advertisement of feminine sanitary napkins (towels) and tampons on television. These advertisements are worth watching when you first arrive so you can choose the product that is best for your needs. Be cautious about trying to wear tampons if you have not done so before; read the product instructions carefully. Tampon insertion for the first time for any woman can lead to some pain, bleeding, or, in rare cases, a shock to your system. Thinner tampons are less likely to break an intact hymen; if you choose not to try them at all, no one will call you a coward. Discard tampon insertion materials in a wastebasket. Used tampons usually may be flushed down the toilet, except in buildings with old plumbing; in that case, they should be wrapped in toilet paper and placed in the trash. Discard used sanitary napkins by wrapping them in toilet paper or small paper bags and placing them in a wastebasket. Never flush a sanitary napkin down a toilet.

DOING LAUNDRY

In our opinion, it is more important to wear clean clothes than expensive ones. Your usual choices for doing laundry include commercial laundries, public laundromats, laundry rooms in dorms and apartment buildings, and home machines. Long-term camping in the wilderness is probably the only situation in which Americans wash clothes by taking them to the nearest stream of running water to pound them on the rocks. Washing clothes "by hand" at home in any convenient sink, tub, or basin with hot water and soap or detergent is always acceptable.

You may need to get used to separating soiled clothing into dark colors and light colors to be washed in separate loads in a washing machine. You can prolong the life of pantyhose and delicate clothing by washing them in small reusable mesh wash bags available in drugstores or grocery stores in aisles where laundry detergents are sold.

Commercial laundries that will handle all clothes cleaning services are available in most places. They provide washing; "dry cleaning" for better clothing; "hand care" for fine clothing such as embroidered, painted, sequined, or silk garments; small repairs; and sometimes even shoe repairs. Most people, however, either

Keeping Clean 75

At the laundromat (Photo courtesy of Marquette University)

wash clothes at home or take them to a self-service public laundromat with coin-operated washers and dryers. Most self-service laundromats sell washing products in one-wash sizes from coin-operated dispensers. You generally have to supply your own baskets (a suitcase will do) to take your clean clothes home. Some laundromats feature "wash-and-fold" services: for a price, an employee will load your clothes into the machines, dry them, and fold them for you to pick up at a specified time.

Most washing machines have instructions on how to use them on the inside of a door or lid. In general, you place your clothes inside, add laundry detergent, select the "cycle" that your load of clothing can withstand, add money if it is a commercial machine, and press or pull a button or knob to start the machine.

If you leave a self-service laundromat while your clothes are washing or drying and do not get back in time to retrieve them from the machine as soon as they are finished, another user is likely to take your wet or dry clothes out of the machine, pile them into a handy basket or no basket, and let them sit on the counter or on the floor awaiting your return. Individual responsibility is the watchword here; if you care for your clothes, stay with them.

You may get the impression from advertisements that getting clothes clean and free of offensive odors is the only thing Americans ever worry about. While most Americans believe that "cleanliness is next to Godliness," TV commercials present an exaggerated perception of the importance of keeping clean. In doing so, they have been successful in making laundry products among the biggest sellers in American supermarkets, spurred on by "soap operas," named for the soap ads often seen on continuing-story episodes on daytime television.

In our opinion, laundry bleach (powdered or liquid bleach products added to the wash water) makes the difference between gray-looking white clothes and bright white clothes. Other laundry products are sold for soaking or treating clothes before washing to remove stubborn stains and for various other purposes. Be careful not to use full-strength bleach for colored fabrics. Try one or two of them and decide for yourself if they perform as advertised.

Hot or very warm water is used to kill disease germs, especially for clothing such as cotton underwear that touches the body directly. Cold water washes are used to keep colors bright on blouses and dresses but are not recommended for heavier items, such as jeans or men's shirts.

Clothes are usually rinsed in clear water after washing, to remove all traces of soap, and then dried. "Fabric softeners" added to the rinse water have a large and loyal following. To keep clothes from clinging to the body after drying, many people use antistatic fabric softeners in the dryer (a common brand is Bounce) during the drying process. Some people find that clothes are softer and smell better if fabric softeners are used, but they are not always necessary.

Drying clothes on a clothesline outdoors is permitted in private "backyards" but will rarely be permitted in apartment buildings. Indoors, clothes can be dried in a mechanical clothes dryer, on a clothesline in the bathroom, or on any other handy device, such as a wooden rack that can be set up in the bathroom and then folded and put away between uses.

Sometimes clothing removed from the dryer is too wrinkled to wear without ironing. You can use an electric iron with or without steam, to smooth out wrinkles by spreading the item of clothing on an "ironing board" (a portable table with legs and a heatproof cover) and rubbing it all over with the hot face of this appliance. All-natural fabrics usually need starch for a quite-perfect look. Use a can of "spray-on" starch on light cottons and silks. It is rare to find an iron and ironing board in a public laundromat, but dorms and residence halls probably have one or more for you to use. Irons can be purchased in department, discount and hardware stores.

Besides washing your personal clothing, separated by type of wash required, you will want to wash larger items such as sheets and towels in large-capacity public machines or one at a time in a home washing machine. Changing bed sheets and pillow cases once a week is standard, more often if required. When in a hotel, towels used after your daily bath or shower will be replaced with clean ones, but at home it may be more convenient to dry and use them more than once before "stuffing" them into the dirty clothes bag.

DUSTING AND VACUUMING

Furniture and other items collect dust, though it may be visible only to your landlady or residence hall captain. Dusting cloths or Handi-wipes can be used once a week on wood or plastic furniture. "Overstuffed" chairs and sofas, covered with fabric, require vacuuming. Living room and bedroom floors and carpets are usually vacuumed, too, but kitchen and bathroom floors that are made of ceramic or other kinds of tile, or linoleum, should be washed with a powdered or liquid disinfecting cleaner and water. Linoleum, wood, and nonceramic tile floors should be waxed occasionally with an appropriate type of wax for protection of the floor and a greater shine.

Brooms and "dust mops" can be used to dust hard-surface floors, but because all they really do is move the dirt around, they are considered less satisfactory for general floor cleaning than vacuuming or washing. Investing in a manual carpet sweeper is a good short-term measure, but it is slow and inefficient. Pretty soon, you will want to use an electric vacuum cleaner.

Vacuums collect the dust by sucking it up into replaceable bags or cups that can later be emptied. Bags must be replaced or cups emptied of accumulated dust and dirt at regular intervals. If you do not have a vacuum of any kind, you can buy one at a discount or department store or borrow one from an obliging neighbor for a morning

Vacuuming

or afternoon of cleaning. But before you borrow that vacuum cleaner, you should be aware that to "borrow" anything puts you under obligations that do not exist in all countries. The assumption is that the item is a physical symbol of the friendship or the relationship you establish with the lender and is to be treated with the same respect you would give your best friend. That means that the item borrowed is to be returned as soon as you are finished with it, in the exact condition, or better, as when you received it, with any damage repaired by you or with a promise to pay to have it repaired. This is assumed to be your obligation.

CLEANING FOR SANITARY PURPOSES

Kitchen appliances such as refrigerators and stoves need regular cleaning to keep them sanitary. Refrigerators should be defrosted manually if they are not the "automatic defrost" kind. To do this, first remove all food from the refrigerator, putting it either in a neighbor's refrigerator or in some sort of portable "cold-keeper," or "cooler," surrounded by ice. (Coolers are normally used to store beer and soft drinks for picnics.)

Now turn the temperature setting to "defrost" or "off" and keep the refrigerator door open a little. Wait for the ice to melt in the freezer section. Remove pieces of ice to a bucket and then to the sink until all the ice is gone, soaking up the water with rags or old towels. Once defrosting is completed, reset the temperature control to "medium," close the refrigerator door, and prepare a bucket of water with vinegar or commercial nonsudsing cleaner in it. Wash the entire inside of the refrigerator, including the walls, shelves, and drawers, with "rags" (cloths) soaked in the water and then wrung out to be wet but not dripping. Use clear water to rinse, and then dry all surfaces with dry rags before restoring the food. We recommend this cleaning procedure be used in the nonfreezer section of automatic-defrost refrigerators about every two months.

Ovens can be cleaned of burned-on food using commercial oven cleaners, carefully following the directions on the product while wearing rubber gloves. "Self-cleaning" ovens use extremely high heat to reduce the burned-on food to ash; the ash can be removed with a wet cloth or sponge after the oven has been allowed to cool. Either process can take most of a day. The difference is that with a self-cleaning oven, the process is mechanical, while the manual cleaning process is labor-intensive, using your labor. Ovens are generally cleaned four times a year, more often if very dirty.

A clean bathroom makes the difference between a healthful living environment and one that could harbor germs that cause illness. Home bathrooms are generally given a good cleaning once a week. It is not considered "lower class" to clean a home bathroom, although American married men tend to leave that chore to their wives. Single men who can afford it often hire cleaning help.

Disinfecting liquids or powders of various kinds, which can be purchased at supermarkets, drugstores, or convenience stores are used for bathroom cleaning. Special toilet-cleaning brushes and rubber gloves are useful to protect your hands. Cleaning products often require a

Cleaning the bathtub

Keeping Clean 81

bucket of hot water in which to dilute the powder or liquid. "Mop pails," which is what these buckets are sometimes called, come with a handle so that moving them about is easier than trying to move a pan. "Wet mops" are used to clean bathroom (and kitchen) floors. Rinsing with clean water is usually required to finish the cleaning process.

Sinks and tubs are cleaned with rags or sponges and cleanser or liquid cleaners, then rinsed and the metal parts wiped dry. Glass windows and mirrors can be cleaned with special glass cleaners that are either sprayed or foamed onto the glass and then wiped clean to remove streaks, but many people believe a solution of vinegar and water sponged on glass and wiped off with newspapers is the best system to avoid streaks.

A clean, shiny, bathroom has a unique glow, and even though it may seem like a dirty job, once it is done, your environment is healthier, safer, and better for you.

CREEPY CRAWLERS

Mickey Mouse may be one of Walt Disney's most famous creatures, but finding a mouse in your kitchen is not going to make you happy. Mice are generally harmless, however. Most American mice are field mice, which come into buildings only to get out of the winter's cold. If you do see a mouse, you can go to your nearest hardware store and buy a mouse trap or two. Bait the traps and put them where the sightings have occurred, checking them frequently to see if they have done their job. When you find a mouse in the trap, put the trap and the mouse in a large paper bag and find an outdoor garbage "dumpster" in which to get rid of them.

Rats are a different story. Rats are larger and meaner and dirtier than mice. If you have rats in your building, it is better to notify your landlord or building maintenance person than to try to get rid of them yourself. If this produces no results, call or write your local government pest control office. Rats carry serious diseases, and their bites can be dangerous. Commercial pest control firms (exterminators) can be hired to get rid of rats and mice, but they tend to be expensive.

From an entomologist's point of view, "bugs" (insects) are fascinating creatures. Your own opinion is probably quite different. Major bug problems will probably be cockroaches, ants, or silverfish (insects that are neither silver nor fish) that live inside and mosquitoes and flies that live outside but want to come inside.

"Roach Motels" are packages filled with roach poison that can be placed at appropriate places around a room or apartment to kill the creatures. Follow the directions on the label carefully. Ants can be killed with poisoned baits. Any drugstore and most supermarkets carry these products. Bug sprays designed for roaches and ants can be fatal if ingested by humans, and should be used only in well-ventilated areas following the directions on the package.

Silverfish live in drawers and in bathrooms that are not cleaned regularly. Special killing agents for silverfish can also be purchased at any drugstore. If the problem persists, you will probably need to notify your building superintendent or call an exterminator.

Mosquitoes and flies are best handled by not letting them come in at all. This usually means putting screens on all windows and doors and repairing rips and holes in existing screens. Hardware stores have special repair kits for holes in screens, but to put in a new screen usually requires a trip to a lumber yard or home improvement store.

"Bug spray" can be sprayed into the air either indoors or outdoors for temporary relief from flying insects. Salves or creams to be rubbed on one's exposed body parts will prevent most bug bites; ask your pharmacist. If you get a mosquito bite, do not scratch it. Use first-aid cream or calamine lotion or ask the pharmacist in the nearest drugstore to recommend a product to relieve the itching.

Bee and wasp stings are more serious than mosquito bites. Many people are allergic to them. If you develop an allergic reaction, request help at the nearest emergency medical center.

You are not likely to encounter all these creatures in your first days in America, but it is good to know how to handle them. The more information you have, the less fear you will experience.

8 Clothing

If your national dress is different from the Western shirt/pants–dress/skirt standard and you are used to wearing it, be aware that it can be your greatest hurdle in cultural adjustment or your greatest asset, marking you immediately as unique and special. Much depends on your own comfort in asserting your identity, how willing you are to be different, and whether there is a financial incentive to change your style of dress or hair length.

Try not to make radical changes in your style of clothing too soon after arrival. Unmistakable foreignness is protection in most surroundings, as Americans are then more apt to excuse behavior that does not fit the norm. In addition, discarding home clothing too early can lead to a crisis of identity at a time when you need all your emotional resources to cope with radical change. You may find assertion in matters of clothing an easy and harmless way to remain outside all social groups until you have observed them and decided which group you wish to be identified with. We advise a wait-and-see course of action for children. The cultural adjustment of children should be based on their obvious feelings toward change or lack of change. Let *them* tell *you* when and if they want to look like everyone around them.

Below is a discussion of the norms practiced in America at present. Whether you choose to follow these immediately, gradually, or not at all is entirely an individual decision. Many new immigrants who do not wish to discard items of clothing of religious or symbolic significance become entrepreneurs so that they do not have to conform to an employer's dress code. This is America; there are always alternatives.

HEADCOVERINGS
One of the major difficulties encountered by people traveling away from their home culture is when and where to show respect by taking off an item of body

covering, such as something worn on the head or feet, or putting on something. Deeply held notions of when and where to cover or uncover a part of the body have caused major cultural clashes throughout history. In our experience, it is usually better to keep to any deeply held home tradition with regard to the head and to follow the local custom with regard to feet.

Headgear that is expected to remain on the head at all times, such as the yarmulke, the turban, the tadung, the chunni, the chador, and the kafiyeh does not cause much comment on the street in larger cities of America. The degree of acceptance in social gatherings drops somewhat, unless cultural exchange is a purpose for the gathering. In the work environment, distinctive dress is seldom tolerated at entry level, but it can be used to advantage in sales positions, making you stand out from other salespeople. Rural areas are more conservative, and you should not be surprised if the reaction to distinctive headgear is negative.

Negative reactions to any foreign dress can range from social tension and silence to distancing and, at worst, attack. Our recommendation is to explain your dress or differences only if you are asked. For example, if you are wearing a kafiyeh or yarmulke or turban and you enter a church where everyone has an uncovered head, you can explain *if someone asks*, by saying, "In our culture, it is the custom to always keep the head covered." Do not add anything else. This statement will indicate that you know that the local custom is different but that you intend to keep your own.

An issue that has been resolved in England and Canada but has yet to be resolved in the United States is the question of whether a turban may be worn as a substitute for a motorcycle helmet. Some states have laws making it illegal to ride a motorcycle without a helmet, but to date, this has not been challenged on the grounds of freedom of religion.

If there is no strong emphasis in your home culture on whether the head must be kept covered, however, and you enter a place where heads are uncovered, you should take off your hat or other headcovering to be polite. If people seem to have their heads covered, you should ask for a temporary headcovering that you can use during your visit. Similarly, if there is no strong emphasis on whether you should take off or put on shoes or slippers in your home culture, and you visit a place where removing shoes is considered customary, the polite thing to do is to remove your shoes.

HAIRSTYLES

Hairstyles are a matter of individual choice within the norms of fashion in the United States. In the 1970s, men in America grew their hair long and had long sideburns. In the 1990s, this is no longer the case. Wearing hair slicked back with oil or brilliantine may be considered "cool" in some circles but may generate disapproval in others. The norm in America is for men to remove facial hair by shaving every day. Neatly trimmed beards and mustaches are acceptable in most areas of the country, though in some professions they may be barely tolerated.

Women are given much more freedom in how they wish to wear their hair, especially through student life. Later, for convenience, most women wear their hair rather short, especially in white-collar professions. However, the main emphasis for both sexes is on keeping one's hair clean and tidy.

Extremely short hair is generally associated with military people and militarylike professions, although it may also be considered fashionable. Extremely long hair is sometimes associated with dancers or professional models. "Permanent waves" are chemically created curls or waves for women whose hair tends to be naturally straight. "Relaxers" are used to create a straighter look for people whose hair tends to be naturally curly. As is true historically, and with most of humanity, it is usually the case that what you are born with seems to be the opposite of what fashion has decreed is "in." To find your own style and stick with it can be a most satisfactory solution regardless of what fashion dictates.

SEASONS AND TEMPERATURES

Throughout the United States, there is a common understanding of the terms summer, autumn, winter, and spring. If your own country's seasons do not correspond to these periods of the year, this can be confusing, so here are the three-month periods and the official dates on which the seasons change in this country:

Summer: June 22-September 23
Autumn: September 23-December 22
Winter: December 22-March 21
Spring: March 21-June 22

Temperatures in the United States are usually measured in degrees Fahrenheit rather than degrees Celsius (Centigrade) and can range from a low of minus 30 degrees Fahrenheit in places like International Falls, Minnesota, in January to a high of 113 degrees Fahrenheit in Phoenix, Arizona, in July (from -34 degrees C to +43 degrees C).

Central heating and air-conditioning can make it difficult to gauge whether one should wear heavy or light clothing, so we recommend that you think of clothing in terms of layers. The higher the temperature, the fewer layers you will need. The lower the temperature, the more you need to wear.

Refer to the chart and map below to help you plan the clothing you should buy for everyday use. They show suitable clothing by region of the country and by season. When we mention "heavy" fabrics in this chart, we mean fabrics such as wool or orlon, as these can substitute for several layers. "Light" fabrics include cotton knits and cotton sweaters, any fabric that allows an air layer to circulate between your skin and the clothing.

If you come from a tropical climate to an American setting anywhere on the East Coast, in the Midwest, or the Rocky Mountain region, we recommend that you wait until you are settled to buy a heavy winter coat. Any coat you buy in your own country will be insufficient, as there are degrees of cold that you will not, at the time, be able to imagine. Once in the United States, look for a "Thinsulate" lined coat for these regions. Such a coat

Necessary Apparel by Region

Region	Seasons
	Autumn ⟷ Winter	Spring ⟷ Summer

East Coast North of Washington, D.C.	Coat　　　　　Heavy coat Sweater　Heavy sweater Slacks　　　　　　Slacks Shirts (long-sleeve) Shirts　　　　Heavy skirts Blouses (long-sleeve) Jeans & T-shirts Dresses (heavy fabrics) Socks or Kneehighs Pantyhose Lt. boots　　　Heavy boots Undershirt 　　　　　Winter underwr	Lt. coat　　　Light jacket Sweater　　　　　Sweater Slacks　　　　　　Shorts Shirts (short-sleeve) Skirts　　　Skirts (light) Blouses (short-sleeve) Jeans & T-shirts Dresses (light fabrics) Socks or Kneehighs Pantyhose Clsd shoes　　Open shoes
East Coast South of Washington, D.C.	Heavy sweater　Lt. coat Slacks　　　　　　Slacks Shirts (long-sleeve) Skirts　　　　　　Skirts Blouses (long-sleeve) Jeans & T-shirts Dresses (medium fabrics) Lt. socks or socks Pantyhose Clsd shoes　　　Lt. boots	Sweater　　　　　Sweater Slacks　　　　　　Shorts Shirts (short-sleeve) Skirts　　　　　　Skirts Blouses (short-sleeve) Jeans & T-shirts Dresses (light fabrics) Lt. socks　　　Kneehighs Pantyhose Clsd shoes　　Open shoes
Great Lakes and Midwest	Coat　　　　　Heavy coat Sweater　Heavy sweater Slacks　　　　　　Slacks Shirts (long-sleeve) Skirts　　　　　　Skirts Blouses (long-sleeve) Jeans & T-shirts Dresses (heavy fabrics) Lt. socks　　　　　Socks Pantyhose Lt. boots　　　Heavy boots Undershirt 　　　　　Winter Underwr	Lt. coat　　　　Lt. jacket Sweater　　　　　Sweater Slacks　　　　　　Shorts Shirts (short-sleeve) Skirts　　　　　　Skirts Blouses (short-sleeve) Jeans & T-shirts Dresses (light fabrics) Lt. socks　　　Kneehighs Pantyhose Clsd shoes　　Open shoes

Necessary Apparel by Region (cont.)

Region		Seasons	
West Coast North of California	Raincoat Heavy sweater Topcoat Slacks Slacks Shirts (long-sleeve) Skirts Skirts Blouses (long-sleeve) Jeans & T-shirts Dresses (medium fabrics) Lt. socks Socks Pantyhose Lt. boots Undershirt	Umbrella Sweater Sweater Slacks Shorts Shirts (short-sleeve) Skirts Skirts Blouses (short-sleeve) Jeans & T-shirts Dresses (light fabrics) Lt. socks Kneehighs Pantyhose Clsd shoes Open shoes	
California and Southwest States	Heavy sweater Lt. coat Slacks Slacks Shirts (long-sleeve) Skirts Skirts Blouses (long-sleeve) Jeans & T-shirts Dresses (medium fabrics) Lt. socks Socks Pantyhose clsd shoes Lt. Boots	Sweater Sweater Slacks Shorts Shirts (short-sleeve) Skirts Skirts Blouses (short-sleeve) Jeans & T-shirts Dresses (light fabrics) Lt. socks Kneehighs Pantyhose Open shoes Open shoes Swimsuits Undershirt	

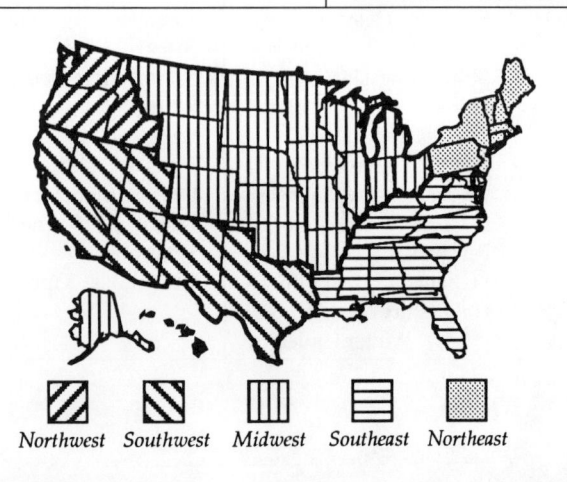

Northwest *Southwest* *Midwest* *Southeast* *Northeast*

Clothing 89

will keep you warm when used over a heavy sweater and is a cheaper alternative to wool, but even that will be insufficient where the temperature goes down to minus 30 degrees Fahrenheit. If the temperature is below 32 degrees Fahrenheit, put on as many layers of heavy clothing as you can. Warm hats, gloves, and scarves are also essential where the weather is cold, as are lined, waterproof boots.

Wear an undershirt. For both men and women in autumn and winter any place in the country north of Washington, D.C., this is an excellent way to continue use of clothing from countries that are not as cold and thus save some money. Undershirts are also used by men in the warmer areas of the country for absorbing sweat.

A snowy day (Photo courtesy of Marquette University)

FASHION

There is a social hierarchy to fabrics. Silk and other 100% natural fabrics, such as cotton or wool, are considered luxury fabrics in the United States; they are likely to cost more than blends of synthetic and natural fibers. Many people are allergic to wool and prefer synthetics, or blends of fibers. One hundred percent polyester, however, has the reputation of being a less than prestigious fabric; it is more acceptable when used in blends to reduce wrinkling.

Leather clothing goes in and out of fashion. Leather sometimes connotes "sexy," as with a very short, tight, woman's leather skirt or a man's tight leather pants. Men's leather jackets, often very expensive and with many zippered pockets, are not usually associated with conservative styles of dress. Leather coats for women are usually considered "high fashion" and compete with fur coats for status. (Animal rights activists are against the wearing of animal skins of any kind, but the fur industry, so far, pays scant attention to their protests.)

Tight clothing, in general, tends to be associated with American notions of what counts as sexy. Americans, however, do not necessarily consider bared shoulders or legs as sexy, with both men and women wearing "tank tops" (sleeveless, U-neck tops), with shorts as routine informal dressing. Bare midriffs used to be considered taboo—especially any baring of the navel—but is becoming more acceptable today. Baring the chest is considered "sexy" behavior for men but is quite acceptable if it occurs in the course of a sporting activity.

Women unused to baring their legs may find that pants are an excellent substitute for skirts, even in business. If you have never worn a skirt, it takes some time to get used to walking in one. American men and women, whether in pants or skirts, are expected to take definite, efficient strides with minimal hip movement and scuffing of the soles of the feet. This is easy to practice in front of a mirror, if you need to, and is an easy way to change people's perception of your personality from passive to active.

The chart above indicates whether closed or open

shoes are appropriate to different seasons. Closed shoes normally include anything from pumps (court shoes) to walking shoes for women to sneakers for both sexes. Open shoes refers to sandals—with heels or without as fits your gender and preference—but rubber "thongs" or "flip-flops" are worn only at the beach or as house slippers. As a new immigrant or foreign student, you can expect to do a great deal of walking in your first few months. Invest in comfortable shoes if you did not bring them with you.

Your choice of a personal style of dressing often goes along with your decisions about the kind of person you wish to be in America. The newcomer has a freedom unknown to most Americans—that of remaking your entire self-image, should you choose to do so; to make a fresh start as if you were reborn. Trying on clothing in different styles, colors, and cuts is sometimes a way to "try on" different personal images until you find one that you would like to adopt. Remember that you can almost always return an item of clothing as long as you have not used it and you have kept your receipt. ("Sale" items are often not returnable.) Have fun in the fitting rooms!

DRESSING FOR DIFFERENT OCCASIONS

Earrings are acceptable for both young men and young women in the 1990s, with earrings standard for older women but not for older men unless they have the panache to carry it off, say, with one small gold hoop in one ear. Other body jewelry, such as nose jewelry for women, is worn only by those at a young, experimental age and marks the wearer immediately as foreign, or "punk," or, at best, "exotic" in some circles. You may decide that your nose ring is an item that attracts people into conversations with you, but there are areas of the country—especially smaller, rural areas—where it can interfere with cultural exchange.

Everyday dressing in America tends to be more casual than in other parts of the world. Many Americans equate wearing national dress with "dressing up" and equate dressing up with wearing a costume. The dignity associated with wearing your customary clothing seems to be lost on most Americans.

Because the definitions of casual, informal, formal and black tie attire vary from culture to culture, refer to the Appendix to understand the meaning of these terms in America.

School and Sports Events

In America, the term "school" refers to everything from high school through college and even postgraduate studies. The dress code for informal events is the same for all these phases of school and for men and women as well: shorts for both men *and* women, jeans, T-shirts or sweatshirts, sneakers, socks, a strong knapsack, and different weights of jackets depending on region and temperature.

People dress in this casual attire at sports events (football, baseball, hockey, and basketball), too, no matter what their age, status, or income level, partly because it connotes egalitarian thinking and partly because sports are mentally associated with informality. As you get more familiar with American clothing, however, you will become aware that some clothes that look very casual cannot be described as inexpensive.

College Graduation

Caps and gowns are worn only on graduation day at American colleges—and only by the participants in the ceremony. Male graduates wear business suits under a graduation gown (tuxedos are worn only if your invitation specifically requests them), and women wear their gown over a dress. This is an occasion when your national dress would be most appropriate from a fashion standpoint, as long as it is also appropriate to the weather that day. If you are attending a graduation ceremony, consult the formal clothing portion of the table in the Appendix.

Small to Medium-Size Businesses

In retail businesses, casual clothing, but not jeans, is the usual attire. In small to medium-size companies, such as software developers or small factories, casual clothing and jeans are permitted for people with no customer contact. Summer shirts are normally short-sleeved (not sleeveless) and winter shirts long-sleeved. Tie widths, belt widths, and accessories like suspenders go in and out of style in each region of the country. Women working for smaller companies are more likely to wear dresses.

Large Businesses

Dress codes, whether written or unwritten, exist in every large company. Men, and women, too, wear business suits for work in larger companies and in any situation where customer contact is expected. Nonprofessional women seldom wear suit jackets; women's suit jackets match skirts and dresses but rarely pants. Skirt length and jacket length vary depending on the prevailing fashion, season, and area of the country. Women wearing slacks (pants) are considered practical or unconventional depending on the industry and company.

Business attire

Blouses with collars are the norm in winter, while collarless blouses are worn in summer. Sleeve length varies depending on weather.

Dark suits are the rule for a job interview with a large corporation for both men and women, with warm or soft colors introduced in the shirt or tie, or, for women, the blouse. Women should wear a suit consisting of a long-sleeved jacket and skirt, not pants. Potential employers expect you to be neat and tidy and to look as eager and businesslike as you can.

Parties

Attire for parties varies greatly depending on the age group, the importance of the people attending, the occasion for the party, the location, and the time of year. The best question to ask your hosts is:

"Should I wear a tie?" (for men)

"Should I wear a dress?" (for women)

If the answer to either question is yes, consult the informal clothing portion of the table in the Appendix. If the answer is no, consult the casual clothing portion of the table.

If a party is formal or black tie, it will be by invitation, and the invitation will specify the dress code. You can then consult the table in the Appendix to get an idea of what is expected.

Theater Outings

Dressing for an evening at an opera, a play, the symphony, or the ballet is another situation in which many factors determine the dress code. If you do not know anything about the production or the size of the theater, play it safe and dress informally.

Family Gatherings

Family gatherings you are invited to, such as Thanksgiving dinner or Christmas day celebrations, are perfect occasions to relax and enjoy yourself by wearing your national attire. Finding you relaxed, your hosts will relax more, too. If, however, you become "part of the family," you will be expected to put on Western dress to accompany the family to various functions.

Funerals
In the past, it was important to dress in black or sober colors for a funeral. However, in the 1990s, one should simply dress in muted sober colors. If the custom is to wear white at funerals in your home country, you should know that older Americans may object to that practice here if the deceased is a prominent member of the community and the funeral is a wintertime event. "Winter white" is associated with festive occasions, fun with snow, and general good times, which makes the wearing of white to a winter funeral inappropriate. Summer funerals, however, seem to have no such prohibition.

SALES
From small boutiques to department stores, discount stores, and used clothing stores, clothing is available in every price range and for every taste, made in every country of the world. There are even ethnic clothing stores in larger cities. To conserve your money, try to purchase items that are "reduced," "marked down," or "on sale." These terms all mean the same thing. The Appendix provides you with a conversion of clothing sizes from metric to U.S. categories.

Sales often correspond to national or local holidays, so that people have time off from work and can go shopping. Refer to the list of important yearly dates and holidays in the Appendix so that you can plan your purchases around those dates. Sales are common in the United States—to such an extent that there are people who are philosophically opposed to paying full price! There is no shame in buying items on sale, even to give as gifts. Unlike food items on sale, clothing sale items do not necessarily have something wrong with them; often they are simply "out of season" and must be sold to make rack space for the fashions of the next season. You will find very soon that the best time for purchasing is after a major gift-giving date, for instance, the day after Christmas.

9 Working in America

America is a capitalist country. This means that American citizens, permanent residents, and anyone cleared by the Department of Labor and the immigration authorities to receive a work permit—male or female—is free to work for money, as much money as he or she can earn. America is also an expensive country. Wages are high, but so are living costs. Americans do not consider it wrong to want material things. As wants become needs, instead of cutting back on expenses, Americans go out and try to make more money by finding someone who is willing to pay them to do something useful.

Not all businesses in America are private enterprises. There are many state and local government enterprises and associations of private individuals that are tax-supported or not-for-profit. Not-for-profit (nonprofit) enterprises pay less than private enterprises, but their main attractions for some people are better job security and benefits.

Workers in America are thought of in two broad categories: "blue collar" and "white collar." Blue-collar workers are people in the skilled trades whose work is primarily manual. White-collar workers are those who work in offices. These are also called "professional" occupations, even though a blue-collar worker may be more of a professional in terms of knowing how to do a job than an entry-level clerk (pronounced as written, not "clark").

Nonprofessionals are usually paid wages, that is, by the hour, and many people feel that they have moved up in life when they make the transition to a salaried position, in which they are paid a set amount every month regardless of the number of hours actually worked. This is often a misperception from a monetary standpoint, however; it is possible to make more money as a plumber in America than as a bank teller, for instance.

Americans work more days than most people in the world. Private companies generally observe only 5 legal holidays a year, and most entry-level jobs allow only 14 days of paid vacation with no options for unpaid vacation. Government jobs and unionized businesses may have better vacation benefits and may even have "sick pay." Office hours are generally 8:00 a.m. to 5:00 p.m. with one hour for lunch, five days a week; these hours are known as "first shift." Some businesses run second and third shifts to work "around the clock." The hourly rate for these shifts is usually higher. Exceptions are jobs in 24-hour convenience stores, which can be low-paying and hazardous.

It is illegal for an employer to knowingly hire an alien unauthorized to work in the United States. An employer is required to verify the alien's identity and authorization to work within three days of employment. As a result, American perceptions to the contrary, not every individual on American soil is free to work for anyone who will hire them.

FOREIGN STUDENTS

Students studying in the United States on a student visa are not allowed to work "off campus" or outside of their college or university for the duration of their educational stay. Does that mean you have to exist only on your student grant or money from home? Not necessarily.

Foreign students are not permitted to sell their labor as an independent contractor (independent business person.) Unlike an American citizen, you may not, for example, tutor individual students on an hourly basis, charge for baby-sitting by the hour, or receive an hourly fee from a university department for consulting assistance, even if you pay taxes on your earnings.

Nevertheless, every campus has part-time jobs that will allow you to earn a few extra dollars without violating your student visa requirements. You are permitted to work on campus up to 20 hours per week while school is in session and 40 hours per week during vacation time as long as you are registered as a full-time student.

Teaching and research assistantships are usually arranged as a part of the application process for graduate students entering most public (state-funded) universities. Private universities have few teaching assistantships, however, and they are mostly arranged after you have paid a semester's tuition. Both jobs require English fluency, but greater fluency is required to teach. If you get a "T.A.-ship," you may be expected to work until the job is done regardless of INS restrictions on hours.

"Networking" (personal contact) is the best method to find out about assistantships. Can you be a research assistant to a professor? Ask the department secretary if a professor needs extra help. Look for work that needs to be done and pays. Consider all opportunities, even those that may not be highly esteemed in your home country. If you cannot find a job that pays, volunteer work can be leveraged into part-time employment on campus after you have shown initiative, persistence and reliability, and as long as you are willing to work for less than a U.S. citizen would be paid.

The first off-campus American job for many foreign students is a full-time job on a training (H-1) visa after they finish their education. The H-1 visa is granted for a 6-month period, which can be extended for an additional 6 months after you graduate. We recommend that you begin your search for trainee employment 8 to 12 months before you graduate. Once you have persuaded an employer to employ you on a training visa, Department of Labor certification is required to attest that the work experience you have been offered cannot be found in your home country. You should request letters for such certification from professors familiar with the type of work you are being offered. Do not be apologetic when requesting these letters; the process is a common occurrence in university life.

PERMANENT RESIDENTS

It comes as a surprise to many that the "green card," the official notice by the federal authorities that you have been accepted as a permanent resident of the United States, is not green! And being accepted for permanent resident status does not mean that you become a U.S. citizen; it means that you are an immigrant with the option to apply for U.S. citizenship and that you have permission to work.

THE JOB SEARCH

To many new immigrants and foreign students, it seems sometimes that the purpose of Immigration and Naturalization Service rules is to place obstacles in the way of precisely the kind of initiative and drive that Americans are proud to recall in their own immigrant ancestry. However, keep in mind that the rules are designed to prevent foreigners from taking work that an American would be willing to perform and to prevent individuals from becoming a "public charge." (To be a public charge means that you are not earning income on your own, that your income comes from government "welfare"—tax money.)

We believe that your attitude toward work will be the single most important factor in your monetary success or failure in America. Look for signs in store windows saying Help Wanted. Tell everyone you know that you are looking for work. Search the classified advertisements in the daily and weekly newspapers.

You respond to an advertisement with a "résumé" (curriculum vitae or bio-data). A résumé is a detailed description of your education and work experience that will tell a potential employer all about you and "sell" your abilities for you. It should include your job or career objective, educational background, work experience beginning with the most current position or organized by the type of work you have performed if you have held many positions, community activities, and awards or certificates you have received. Keep working on your résumé until you, your teachers, and your sponsors are convinced it actually describes what you are capable of doing in a favorable light but with no exaggeration.

Letters of reference from former employers or teachers—whether at your university in America or in your home country—are always helpful. However, the content of an American letter of reference is a little different from that used in many other countries. The letter should call your prospective employer's attention to your ability, not your ancestry. It should discuss your specific achievements as an individual while on the job and not make vague expressions of goodwill and friendship with your family. It should be typed and should provide the name, address, and telephone number of the person writing it in case your prospective employer wishes to check your references.

For jobs that require designing or writing, a better reference than anyone's letter from the old country is a portfolio showing samples of your work. Do not send this to a prospective employer; take it with you to present at the time of an interview.

One dilemma you will face is a dilemma all job seekers face, whether American or foreign: employers seem to want only experienced personnel, but how does one gain experience? Just remember this: you need only one job. The United States is an evolutionary society and you will find your "niche" (pronounced *nitch*) eventually, one that matches your skills with the work there is to be done. Perfect your English language speaking skills, and be ready to do any honest work. Just do not give up.

A dilemma specific to foreigners is lack of American work experience and the probability that you will not stay around for the long term. Why should an American for-profit enterprise spend time and money to train you? Here is where you might offer volunteer labor to get a foot in the door. Your volunteer labor—call it an "unpaid internship"—will result in some American experience. After a volunteer period of a few months—we would say two months, maximum—in which you have shown your willingness to work hard and intelligently, you can often overcome an employer's reluctance to employ you. Rely on building personal relationships of trust and mutual respect with a prospective employer; a willingness to expect less pay than a U.S. citizen does not hurt either.

Make a list of the entry-level jobs in your field. Do you have the educational requirements to apply for them? (For clerical and even some professional jobs you do not always need to know how to do the job advertised, but you need to know the technical jargon of the industry or its way of thinking in order to succeed.)

If you want to find an entry-level professional position, start with the Yellow Pages of the telephone book to find employers in your field with offices close to your place of residence. Call managers of different companies and ask them to see you to discuss present and future opportunities. Do not restrict yourself to the city you are in; be open to all opportunities for honest work, and use a small job as a stepping-stone to get to a better one.

Sales jobs are the usual entry-level openings. But how should you choose one to apply for? Americans are some of the world's best salespeople, and some salespeople get commissions if they recruit more salespeople. There is no social stigma to selling; however, there is a sales hierarchy that is not commonly acknowledged. The rule of thumb is the higher the value of the item, the higher the social status of the salesperson. You will find that partners of prestigious accounting, legal, and real estate firms are salespeople, too; they just sell higher-priced services. Conversely, selling candy in a convenience store is not as prestigious as selling hardware on the floor of a hardware store.

If you want a job in government, you may have to take a Civil Service examination, and for some of those jobs you must be a U.S. citizen. Call your city, state, or county's Job Service office for information.

Reply quickly to job advertisements in the paper, with an original cover letter for each application. Be positive about past job experiences, never talk against a past employer, and stay cheerful. Employers want people who will fit in with their team and get along with everyone. If you are more of a "loner" than a team player, stay away from selling and from large corporations. Look, instead, for a new business that wants creativity.

How do you stay clear of "con-artists" and shady deals? Here are our recommendations. Do not deal with anyone whose source of income is a mystery either to you or to people who know that person. Also, do not deal with a person whose life-style and spending habits are far beyond the income level you would expect a successful person in this field to afford. (Ask an American for this evaluation, if necessary.) Do not agree to sell a product you do not understand. For example, you may be able to sell a million shares for a mutual fund, but if you do not know what it is investing in and who is managing its investments, you should not agree to sell for them. Any job for which you are not required to either show output or be present and working is probably questionable.

Check with your local Better Business Bureau, a nonprofit corporation that keeps records of illegal practices and complaints against business and charitable organizations, before you decide to do business with or work for an organization. Better Business Bureaus register and investigate written complaints and can arbitrate consumer disputes, too.

If you have a strong non-European accent we do not recommend trying to reach a prospective employer by telephone. However, if you do not have a strong non-European accent and you do not get a call from an employer granting you an interview, call the person to whom you sent your résumé, usually the "Human Resources" manager, and ask if your application has been received and if someone can tell you its status. Ask for an interview on the telephone if the person is too busy to see you in person. Practice interviewing by role-playing with a friend.

INTERVIEWING

In chapter 8, we discussed the type of clothing appropriate for professional interviews. If you are going for an entry-level nonprofessional job, it may be acceptable to wear casual clothing but not jeans. Sleep well the night before your interview. Eat a good breakfast. Do not smoke at all that day if you possibly can; American companies are aiming toward a smoke-free environment.

Be confident. This is not the only job or employer in the country, but be there 15 minutes early. Check your appearance just before the interview. Blow your nose, tidy your hair, eat a breathmint, and do not panic. When you meet the interviewer, shake hands firmly. Speak clearly and understandably. Smile.

If you come from a country where it is not polite to look people in authority in the eyes, be careful. You can ruin an interview in America by not looking someone in the eyes; Americans view it as a sign of dishonesty or timidity. If you are unused to looking a person in the eyes, focus on a spot between the interviewer's eyebrows. This looks to the interviewer as if you are focusing on his or her eyes while you maintain your custom.

If you come from a culture where being part of a good group was highly valued, be aware that you may be disposed to say, "The group I was in did..." more than "I did..." Americans value team orientation in some of the newer professions (software development, for example) but are not likely to consider it a plus when evaluating an individual. If you say you managed or built a team, that is another story.

People from older civilizations have a common misperception of the purpose of an interview. You may have the idea that the purpose is to "get to know you," and this is often a phrase used when the interview is arranged. However, in America, the purpose is not to get to know the *whole* you—meaning all of your achievements to date, your family's status, your intentions for the future, what your political persuasions are, and so on—but to find out if you will be able and willing to do the job. Do *not*, therefore, discuss anything that is not relevant to that central point; you should not waste the interviewer's time.

Another common problem faced by newcomers who have been through a tremendous amount of change in a short time is that you may be more in need of someone to talk to (a friend or a psychiatrist) than an interview. No matter how tempting it is to talk about your feelings and insecurities, your reaction to America and Americans (positive or negative), this is *not* the time or place for such a discussion, even if the interviewer is interested, because it can lead you to disclose more than you planned to. Keep to the central point; the organization has a need, you are willing to fulfill it.

You should ask some questions about any topic that is not mentioned in the advertisement or by the interviewer.

- What is the job? What are the daily duties expected?
- If you have not researched the market value of the job, ask, "Are this company's pay scales competitive in the industry?" This brings salary into the conversation.
- Will you be paid a salary or wages? (Wages are paid per hour.) How much and how often? (Figure that 30% of your salary will be withheld for taxes and about 10% for Social Security and Unemployment Compensation.)
- Are there flexible hours, or does this job require that you be at a desk from 8:00 a.m. to 5:00 p.m.?
- Is health insurance part of your compensation package? If so, will you be eligible for coverage immediately? What is the deductible? Will a portion of your earnings go to pay health insurance or will the company pay all of the premium?
- Will you be eligible to participate in a retirement plan or profit-sharing plan?
- Will you be allowed to work more hours one day in order to take some time off another day? (This is called compensatory or "comp" time.)
- Is there any overtime pay? (Overtime pay in America is usually "time and a half," meaning 1½ times your hourly rate.)
- What is the next level of pay and title that you can work toward? What is required of you to achieve that? How long does it take an entry-level person, on average, to be promoted to the next level? How many people has the company promoted from this position in the last year?

While an interviewer may ask you about your age, your marital status, how many children you have or plan to have, your race, your religion, your ethnic group, or your medical history, none of that information may be used to discriminate against you in offering or not offering you a job. (This rule applies regardless of whether you are a permanent resident or a U.S. citizen.) The dividing line between asking for simple information and asking with intent to discriminate is so fuzzy that if you believe the interviewer is asking you questions that would not be asked of every applicant, you might consider reporting him to your local Equal Opportunity office.

At the end of the interview, thank the interviewer, and ask for his or her business card if you have not been given one already. You will probably be told that someone will call you when a decision has been made. (The phrase "Don't call us, we'll call you," is a cliché.) However, it is not impolite to ask when a decision will be made. Write a letter after the interview, thanking the interviewer for taking the time to meet with you and restating how your experience is relevant to the job. Be upbeat and positive in the letter, saying you are looking forward to a favorable response. Even if the interview did not go as well as you planned, do not apologize for anything you said or did. But if you forgot to mention an achievement or some positive idea, put it in the thank-you letter.

If you have been to a number of interviews and are being told you are "overqualified for this job," it means you need to revise the qualifications (credentials) you are presenting to prospective employers, or, if you feel you can handle it, search for a higher-level position. It is tempting to list all of your degrees, particularly if you have had to redo your professional education in the United States; be careful not to list more qualifications than an advertised job requires. Prepare a few different versions of your résumé for different levels of jobs and send the prospective employer only the level of qualifications that would be needed for that job. Ask an American in the same profession to evaluate the job for the level of qualifications required, if necessary.

BUYING A JOB

Employment agencies are businesses that try to match employers with potential employees. There are three basic types. The first is the general employment agency, which usually does more business when the employment situation favors the employer, that is, when jobs are hard to find, and collects a fee from the job seeker. The second is the so-called headhunter agency, which collects a fee from the employer for finding people with very specific skills. The third is the "temporary help" agency. These firms contract with employers to provide employees (cynically referred to as "bodies") for specific, usually short periods. Your pay will come from the agency, not the employer, and the better you are at fitting various job requirements, the more jobs you will be given.

Some agencies are not as honest as they should be and collect fees from you, the job seeker, without ever intending to find you a job. Others have an unstated practice of collecting fees from both the job seeker and the employer. Be careful! Talk with an experienced friend, if possible, before you attempt to use a commercial employment agency. Better agencies are those where only the employer is paying the fee. Agency fees are percentages based on the amount you would be paid per year.

Another means of buying yourself a job is to join the army, the navy, or the air force. You trade your efforts and a promise to go to war, if necessary, for moderately good pay, job security, and benefits. While the military does not have the same prestige as a job in the private sector (nothing in America is viewed quite like a white-collar job), it is a fair trade. If you are not a U.S. citizen, however, joining the U.S. military can be grounds for your home country to revoke your citizenship. In addition, to continue in the military after the first term of enlistment or to become an officer, the U.S. government requires that you become a U.S. citizen. Ask yourself the question: Could you fight for the United States if America goes to war against your home country?

TECHNICAL SKILLS

Manual labor is valued in the United States almost as highly as intellectual labor, and you may find it to your benefit to start your career in a job with a higher manual content, for instance, in a restaurant, and work your way up. Do not expect to start at the top; see it from an employer's point of view. However, once you are a permanent resident, be aware that you do not have to settle for less than a U.S. citizen in terms of working conditions or benefits.

If you come from a country where time and people are abundant, you will need to get used to the idea that *your* time is valuable and can be sold. You can place a classified advertisement in a newspaper offering your services. You might offer bookkeeping services, or offer to prepare tax returns for April 15 of each year, the date by which income tax payments are due. Are you good at reading palms or at astrology? While highly educated individuals sometimes scoff at the ability of such people to be accurate, it is usually not illegal to offer such services if people are willing to pay for your advice. Advertise your services for a fee per session. As far as the market is concerned, an expert is someone who has spent more time than anyone else around studying a particular subject or practicing a particular skill.

Can you work with wood or do plumbing repairs? Repair automobiles or electrical appliances? Can you cook? Can you cut and style hair or give manicures? Program a computer? Are you good with children? With growing plants? Can you sew? Drive a car? Can you add up a column of numbers, with or without a calculator, faster than most people? These abilities are valued as accomplishments no matter who does them. While most people do their own minor repairs at home, those with special skills can always find work doing things that others cannot.

It is possible to apprentice yourself to a barber, a hairdresser, or a manicurist to learn their trade. Technical colleges offer practical (vocational) training along with educational courses. You may find an introductory course about computers useful; even low-skill jobs often require you to use a computer. Highly skilled occupations, such as tool-and-die maker, color-press lithographer, and nursing, can also be entered through technical college programs and then apprenticeships.

Equivalency requirements for professional occupations such as engineer, physician, attorney, or dentist are set on a state-by-state basis. That means that requirements in New York State, for example, may be different from requirements in Texas or California. Generally, English-language skills (spoken and written) are set at a very high level, and current technical knowledge is required. For many professions, this can mean several years of redoing some or all of one's college education. How many American courses you may have to take depends on the profession, where you come from, and your persuasive powers. Several professional occupations now have associations of foreign graduates who try to lobby for changes in regulations for accreditation; for instance, there is a Foreign Medical Graduates Association. A library reference source called the Gale *Encyclopedia of Associations* can help you find out where your professional organization has its national headquarters; then you can write or call for information on the requirements set by the states you are interested in.

You may decide after checking the job market and interviewing and perhaps even being offered a job or two, that you do not want to work for anyone, or that you would like to maintain your differentness from the mainstream beyond the point acceptable to most employers. What then? One option is to market your skills to a number of different clients. A second and perhaps related option is to start your own business. If you buy a business, you should expect to pay anyone who works in it—including family. Including women. In addition, as soon as there is even one employee who is not a family member, fairness demands that family members should have to work to prove themselves to the same extent as nonfamily employees.

ON THE JOB IN CORPORATE AMERICA

If you take a job working for a large corporation, you become the newcomer in the organization. Be prepared for some of the same problems you might have experienced in being a newcomer to the country. The group you enter has a certain way of doing things; you have to find out what those ways are and adjust your

On the job in corporate America (Courtesy of Northwestern Mutual Life Photo)

behavior as necessary to get the job done without agreeing to change your personality or compromise your principles.

For all you hear about the competitiveness and individualism in America, society works on trust, agreement, and compromise here just as it does in other cultures. Agreements must be to the advantage of all parties. A good test is: Would I accept this if it was offered to me? And when someone makes you an offer, ask: Would you be willing to agree under the same terms you are offering me?

Working in American corporations can bring a heady sense of personal achievement, especially if you come from a country in which inefficiency is a rampant malaise. Most Americans are "open to new ideas" and believe everything can be improved, especially people. Americans are always taking courses and seminars to learn new skills or to refresh their professional knowledge or simply stay current in their field. Several professions that require licenses to practice, such as law, medicine, and education, have requirements for continuing education.

An observation of most newcomers from older civilizations is that there is no system of apprenticeship in American companies. The value placed on youth and on everything being new and different is one that served the country very well when the method for every task needed to be invented from scratch. It has resulted, however, in a philosophy of continuous upheaval—and continuous creativity—so that instead of passing knowledge and techniques from people who have been in the corporation for a few years to the new people, American companies seem to "reinvent the wheel" repeatedly. The problem is that there may be only five or six ways to make a wheel profitably, and maybe someone already discovered all those ways in the same company a few years ago. Without a teaching-by-example tradition that knowledge gets lost and results in wasted time and effort. But, it forces people to think about why they are doing something rather than of what they are doing.

Americans on the job can give you the impression they are not conscious of hierarchy; everyone calls everyone by first names, after all, and office doors are usually left open. But hierarchy exists. Watch the order in which people sit down (most important first, at the head of a table), the relative size of offices and desks (the larger they are, the more important the person), the amount of space around people (the higher the person's rank, the wider the space and the broader their gestures), the body language (the larger the ego, the more relaxed the limbs), and who is allowed to smoke (the boss). However, in a well-run company, communication flows from bottom to top as well as top to bottom, and the "grapevine" or "rumor mill," which acts as the informal horizontal communication channel in a company, tends not to be overly active.

As a foreigner trying to make friends, try to emphasize similarities rather than differences. When you are new in an American company, people expect you to introduce yourself. Yes, this is the opposite of what is considered polite in Europe or in Asia, but it should not be interpreted as being rude. You are on social probation, and until you have "paid your dues" and shown that you have the ability and trustworthiness you said you have, you will not be considered part of the group. Most Americans have ways to speed up the acceptance process when they are newcomers: sports talk, sharing activities after work, emphasizing similarities at every point. You can, too. It may just take you longer. We suggest you avoid group events until you have formed some individual relationships; our admittedly unscientific observation is that it is easier for people to act on xenophobia or racism when protected by group anonymity.

The main criticism of foreign-born employees by their co-workers is usually that they work too hard. This sometimes results in being popular with either your co-workers or your employer but not both. You can avoid this by striking a balance so as to be liked and trusted by both groups; work hard but within regular hours.

Although America no longer practices legal apartheid, it is still a society psychologically separated by race and color. People have the freedom to choose where they live and work and who they give a job to, and the choices they make reflect their biases, racial and otherwise. The civil rights movement of the 1960s brought legal rights to African-Americans, but there has been little economic progress for them. It may come as a shock to many Asian and Hispanic newcomers that African-Americans may not view them as fellow minorities but instead as a threat to their livelihood. Be aware of these concerns in your dealings at work. Many feelings remain inarticulated, sometimes because people cannot express them. Treat people with dignity, and expect the same in return.

All people, including women, must be treated with dignity. Male newcomers from more patriarchal cultures are often unsure of how to treat professional women in an office environment. The answer is simple: Women should be treated as professional people—not dolls, not invalids, not property, not slaves—whether they are single or married, old or young. If you are unsure of how to address a woman, *ask*.

About the only difference you should observe between men and women on the job is that men do not swear in front of women. But this, too, is a convention that is breaking down. Women are likely to rise to greet customers and to shake hands like men do in most business meetings, and they no longer wear drab and dull colors so as not to attract attention to their femininity. If you are from a culture where bright colors mean a woman is available, you should know that bright colors have no such meaning here. Assuming a woman must be a secretary if she works for a large corporation could be viewed as an insult if the woman has more authority. Major insults, whether you are foreign or not, include expecting a woman to make the coffee, expecting any woman present to take minutes at a meeting, ignoring a woman's contribution to a conversation or a project, or, worse, ascribing such a contribution to male influence.

If you have been accustomed to seeing male secretaries in a work environment, it may surprise you to discover that they are a rare sight in corporate America. There is a perception that male secretaries are homosexuals; it is a stereotype that is difficult to break. As a result, males performing secretarial tasks are given gender-neutral titles such as administrative assistant or clerk.

If you are a female newcomer to America, do not expect American men to make any concessions to your sex. But you are entitled to the same treatment as that expected by American women. Women in America walk in front of a man in passing through a doorway and in front of a man when being escorted or ushered anywhere. Speak up in meetings even when men are present. Read and know your company's sexual harassment policy. Sexual harassment is a legal offense as well.

Sexual Harassment and Sexual Assault
Sexual harassment is defined as an unwelcome sexual advance or request for sexual favors by a person in a position of higher power in a relationship. For instance, if an instructor promises a student a better grade in exchange for sexual favors, even when there is consent, or an employer makes a romantic relationship a condition of promotion, that constitutes sexual harassment. Sexual harassment is illegal; if you feel pressure of this nature, you can complain to your local Equal Opportunity office.

Newcomers should be warned that it is easy to misread sexual signals in an early stage of adjustment. If you feel you have been harassed, we suggest you consult a few Americans to see if the circumstances you describe would be viewed as sexual harassment by mainstream American standards. The true test will be the answer to the questions: Did you say no? Did the person then continue without your assent? If so, you probably have grounds for complaint and redress.

Sexual assault, or forced physical relations, is punishable with imprisonment, the length of which varies based on the legal system's evaluation of the seriousness of the offense.

Settling into Your Job
If you are asked to set short-term goals and long-term goals, and you are from an older culture, your concept of short term is likely to be in the five- to ten-year range, and your concept of long term is likely to be twenty to thirty years. Americans usually mean six months to one year when they say "short-term" and about three years when they say "long-term."

Use your first few months on the job to observe company policy in action. Be suspicious of a company whose actions do not match its policy and internal statements. As an example, companies that do government work have to have Affirmative Action policies, and some places need "front" people—minorities in whose name they can get government contracts. Long Affirmative Action policy statements accompanied by entry-level affirmative action but no minorities in the higher ranks are good indications that a company is "window-dressing," or hiring minorities without any intention to promote them. You don't have to be part of this kind of charade unless you wish to be. This *is* a free country, as long as some people are willing to stand up and say no.

So, when you hear the words, "You're hired," celebrate! You are surviving just fine. You can quit if you find something better, or if you do not like this job. In America, you can be as monetarily successful as *you* choose to be.

10 Buying a Vehicle

Buying an automobile (auto or car), truck, or van is a rite of passage for most Americans, marking their entry into adulthood or the middle-class world of independence and mobility. For a newcomer, it is simply a matter of answering these questions: Do you need a car? If you have a job that requires you to own a car, or if your area is without convenient public transportation, you will need a car. Can you afford to purchase one? In addition, can you afford insurance, gas, and maintenance for the car you buy? If you know absolutely nothing about cars and do not wish to learn, or find yourself needing to buy a car in the northern part of the country with winter approaching, consider a new car.

Unlike many countries, you do not need to have the full purchase price of the car to buy one; all you need to have is the money for a "down payment." The down payment is usually around 20 percent of the car's value. The rest can be obtained from a bank, a leasing or finance company, or the car dealer as a secured loan with the car as collateral. What this means is that if you do not make the monthly payments on the car, the lender may "repossess" the vehicle, that is, take it away from you.

Everyone cannot afford a new car—even in America. So for most young people and newcomers, a used car is the best option. Used cars are advertised in the classified section of the newspaper, but in addition, almost all new car dealers have a lot full of used cars that you can choose from. If you are not familiar with the different models of cars offered, you will need to do some research and reading or ask for assistance from people who have been here longer. Every person has a personal preference for a car company or model. An objective assessment is available from the American Automobile Association (AAA) publications, *AAA Autotest* and the *AAA Car Buyer's Handbook*. These are available to AAA members and nonmembers at any of AAA's offices throughout the country.

A nonprofit organization called Consumers Union has publications that advise not only on prices but also on the test results of different makes and models and on how to negotiate with a dealer. To get a copy of its *New Car Buying Guide* or *Used Car Buying Guide*, write to Consumer Reports Books, 9180 Le Saint Drive, Fairfield, OH 45014-5452, or call 1-513-860-1178, or check with your local library.

Once you have narrowed your search to the makes and models of the cars you would like to see, the next decision is usually whether you should lease or buy the car. Leasing is long-term car rental; the ownership of the car remains with the leasing agency. When you purchase a car, ownership passes to you at once. To make a decision whether to lease or buy, you will need to compare the payments based on leasing and the total amount you would pay in interest, to the payments and total interest amount you would pay under a purchase financing arrangement. Auto leasing and financing rates fluctuate a great deal, so you have to shop around; get the best rates and then do your comparison.

GETTING A CAR LOAN

A new or used car in good condition may be used as security for a loan from a bank or credit union. When a car is security for a loan, the bank can repossess it if you fail to make the monthly loan payments. Car dealers finance cars, too, but their interest rates are usually higher. We recommend that you bargain for a good purchase price first and then bargain separately for a low interest rate if your car dealer is the lender. Your banker can give you an idea of the price that a dealer should be asking for a new or used car by looking up standard pricing information for you.

The best time of the year to buy a car is toward the end of September. At that point, the new models for the next year are arriving on the lot, and the dealer has to get the last year's models off the lot. It is the best time to make a deal.

Once you have bought your car, you have to get it registered in your name for proof of ownership, and register it anew in any state you move to. Contact a car insurance company or AAA for insurance coverage related to accidents and third-party liability. Motor vehicles have to pass an emission test once a year.

BASIC CAR CARE
Most of us get along quite well without knowing much about the inside of a car or even how it works. All you have to know to survive with your car is how to pump gas (petrol), get the oil checked, where to take it for maintenance, how to use a car wash, and what to do in case of breakdowns or accidents. Beyond survival, there are volumes of books, even courses and radio call-in shows, dedicated to discussing car problems and solutions. It is, in short, an American preoccupation, so there is no shortage of information.

Many newcomers have a problem with the self-service procedure for pumping gas. In some gas stations you are expected to pay the cashier first and then pump the gas. In others, you pump first and pay later. There is a higher price for "full serve" (when someone else pumps gas into your car for you) in comparison to "self-serve" (when you pump the gas yourself). Signs will indicate which pumps are which. At most gas stations, you can pay by cash, debit card, or credit card, and in some parts of the United States, there are gas pumps that allow you to run your plastic card through a card reader for payment so that you do not have to pay a live person. Impersonal but efficient.

To learn how to check oil in the car, take your car to a full-serve station and have the attendant show you how to check the level on the oil stick. Check the oil gauge in the car frequently; do not let it fall below the danger zone.

In the northern areas of the country, your car will need winterizing and antifreeze when the temperature gets below freezing: 0 degrees Centigrade, 32 degrees Fahrenheit. Use a can of Heet or alcohol to absorb water in the gasoline. Drive slowly—very slowly—in snow.

Many gas stations have service centers and mechanics

Pumping gas

who work there to fix cars. These are lower-cost alternatives to taking the car back to your car dealer's service center when it needs servicing or repair, but they cannot fix everything, and if a part needs replacing, they may refer you to a dealer. It depends on what is wrong with the car. Regular maintenance such as tune-ups, winterizing, and oil changes are gas station service center specialties.

For breakdowns and emergency road service, you can call a nearby towing company or gas station and tell them where you are. Towing and on-site repairs are expensive; AAA or other auto club memberships include towing insurance in case your car breaks down. AAA basic road service includes 24-hour-a-day on-site assistance to fix flat tires, to jump start rundown batteries, to open car doors when you have locked yourself out, to get your car out of ditches and snowbanks, or to deliver gas when your car runs dry. If you are in the northern part of the country and have never driven in snow, sleet, or storms, we strongly recommend emergency road service coverage.

CAR SAFETY

Remember to buckle your seat belt every time you get into your car; most states have seat belt laws and fines for noncompliance. Lock your car whenever you leave it, even if you are leaving only for a very short time. *Never* leave the keys in the ignition. Roll up the windows so that no one can reach in and open the door, and cover all packages that might be seen through the window. If you live in a high crime area, ask a car mechanic to tell you which essential part you might remove so as to make it impossible for a thief to drive away with your car. If you live in an area where car stripping is common, you may need to buy special locking stud nuts to prevent your wheels from being removed and a special antitheft lock assembly and plate. Keep a copy of your car registration papers and serial number at home, not just in the car.

If you are driving alone, roll up all your windows and lock the door opposite you. Keep your car in good condition to minimize breakdowns. Check your gas tank before driving anywhere. Never stop for a hitchhiker, no matter how well dressed. Muggers have been known to play on your sense of pity, so we advise you not to stop for anyone whose car appears to have broken down. Instead, stop at the nearest phone and call the Highway Patrol (traffic police or sheriff) to report the breakdown. That is the best help you can provide.

At night, avoid parking in any spot that will not allow a clear view of your car as you return to it. Take your keys out of your pocket or purse before you leave a building to return to your car; do not fumble for them in the dark in an isolated parking lot. Check your car to make sure no one is in the back seat before you get in; when you get in, lock the door from the inside immediately.

If your car breaks down, do not accept help from anyone who stops. Stay in your car, roll up the windows, and lock the doors. If someone offers to help, ask them to stop at a phone and call for help—your motor club, the nearest service station, or the police—and if they genuinely wish to help you, they will.

If you suspect that you are being followed, do not drive to your home. Drive to the nearest police station, hospital, or fire station, and when you get there, do not get out. Stay in your car and honk the horn.

CAR THEFT

If your car is stolen, you must report the theft to the police. They will need to know the car's serial number and the make, model, and year of manufacture to try to get it back. If you do not have a copy of your car registration and serial number because it was in the car that was stolen, call the dealer who sold it to you. If your car was insured, contact the insurance agent. Insurance companies will pay on a theft policy if you have informed the police in a timely manner.

ACCIDENTS

The first rule to remember is that you should not leave the scene of an accident. Stay with your car, and be prepared to exchange driver's license and insurance information with other people involved or the police if they are called. Make sure you obtain the name of the insurance company providing coverage for anyone who has damaged your car.

The first thing that happens after anything worse than a "fender bender" (minor accident) is that someone calls the police—and ambulances if necessary—who arrive and assess the damage. The police fill out an accident report describing what happened as objectively as possible. If there is damage, you and the other party to the accident will be asked for the names of your respective insurance companies. Cars may need to be towed out of the way and to service stations for repair, and statements will be taken from each person involved. If you were driving and someone with you was hurt, you or your insurance company can be sued for damages. After the accident, the police may record a traffic violation and someone may get a ticket.

Be careful not to accept blame for causing the accident, even if you are quite sure you may be at fault. The reason is that it is best to leave it to those who are in authority to decide the issue. Your insurance company has to pay damages if you are at fault, anyway. That is what insurance is for. Your insurance company may raise your premium thereafter, but you can deal with that situation later. Some states require "no-fault" insurance that brings the issue down to how much damage was done and what it will cost to fix it rather than whose fault it was.

Do not avoid the police. If you are injured, the insurance company of the other party should pay for your medical bills. If it refuses, get yourself a personal injury lawyer to make sure your rights are protected. Personal injury lawyers work on a "contingency fee" basis in almost all states. This means they do not get paid a fee in addition to their expenses unless they obtain a monetary judgment in your favor. You have a right to representation and justice whether or not you are a citizen of the United States.

Do not sign any releases that insurance adjusters may want until you are certain you have *no* injury. Insurance adjusters try to get to the people in an accident before they decide to contact personal injury lawyers, so you should allow a few days after the accident to decide for yourself if you are injured. Go to a doctor if you feel unwell even if you do not have health insurance and have to pay the fee.

11 Health and Medical Care

While getting sick is not fun anywhere in the world, in the United States it can be a newcomer's nightmare. America does not have a national health care system administered by the government. You will find a patchwork of physicians, clinics, hospitals, licensing authorities, government assistance programs, medical corporations, and trade associations regulated by state agencies and subject to wide fluctuations in quality of care and competence.

Other than local government clinics, in an entrepreneurial society such as the United States, health and medical care organizations intend to make a profit, although some facilities may be nonprofit and tax exempt. Many clinics and hospitals are now owned by large public corporations, which employ physicians in their chains of "emergency" clinics or "specialty shops."

ROUTINE HEALTH CARE AND FITNESS

For routine care in America, health care and medical care, while referred to almost interchangeably, are drifting apart as we approach the end of the twentieth century.

The term "health care" now often refers to the practice of good hygiene, prevention of illness, and "wellness," or keeping the body (and mind) in good shape. "Medical care" refers to the care given by physicians, surgeons, dentists, nurses, and other medically trained personnel, the kind of help you look for if you think you are sick.

Health care is offered by most clinics connected with local (city or county) government. Public health nurses give "shots," or injections, for travelers, take blood pressure readings, and often act as a referral service to other medical personnel. Local people sometimes refer to these clinics as "free" clinics, but they are not totally free; some payment, though small, is usually required.

Most Americans are conscious—more conscious, perhaps, than people of other cultures—of maintaining healthy habits and a healthy regimen of diet and exercise. For example, you will find a profusion of weight-loss clinics that appear to be part of the medical profession but are not; scientific-sounding names are an effective marketing technique.

Exercise is a natural way to stay healthy, and the many university recreational centers, county parks, nonprofit health clubs, and community centers ensure that you can get as much exercise as you were used to in your home country or as much as your body needs. Look for a YMCA or YWCA in your area. If you do not know how to use the exercise machines in the "workout" room of these health clubs, ask for an instructor to demonstrate each one so that you use them safely and effectively.

Swimming pools in America are "coed," that is, for both men and women. The practice varies for steambaths, saunas, and jacuzzis. However, just about everywhere in the country, men and women have separate changing rooms. Women's changing rooms generally do not have separate stalls; if you object to changing in full view of other women, you can use a toilet stall for privacy.

SMALL PROBLEMS

When you have time to decide where to go for medical help and the illness appears ordinary, like a cold, a slight rash, or a mild stomach ache, students use the facilities of their university or college medical clinic. Others use "walk-in" clinics, also called "minor emergency" clinics. If a clinic is closed, any pharmacist (chemist) can suggest what are called "over-the-counter" medications. These are medicines for mild problems, available to anyone on open shelves for the price of the medicine alone. Pharmacists will also advise you, if asked, which medicine is preferred for the particular problem you are experiencing.

Cultures differ in their reference to the part of the body in which the discomfort exists. To be precise, point directly to an area that hurts rather than using words.

Powerful medicines cannot be sold by just anyone but must be prescribed by a physician (except in Florida, where a pharmacist may prescribe medications). They must be compounded by a licensed pharmacist to the specifications written on the prescription, then paid for in the pharmacy, or drug store, or delivered to your home and paid for on delivery. To save money, ask your pharmacist if there is a "generic" (no brand-name) drug that can be safely substituted for the brand-name drug the doctor prescribed.

FINDING A DOCTOR

Physicians in America may be male or female. Female physicians and male physicians examine both men and women (adults and children). If this is not acceptable, you may request a physician of the preferred gender, although some referrers may give you a bit of an argument.

Doctors range in experience from traditional healers found in many transplanted cultures to the latest graduate of the most prestigious, technologically sophisticated medical schools in the world. If you trust those with the latest in Western medical knowledge and skills, you will look for a medical doctor (physician) affiliated with a hospital in the area. The best recommendation is from someone who knows you, your personality, and your culture; ask a friend to suggest a doctor who would suit you. Better still, ask a nurse. Foreign students can ask the university health clinic personnel for a referral to a long-term doctor.

Physicians advertise in the Yellow Pages telephone directory or subscribe to Physician Referral Services. You could also call the most convenient hospital to request some names and telephone numbers of local "general practitioners" (GPs). General practitioners will refer you to a specialist if necessary. Get several recommendations so that you have a few alternatives if you do not feel confident of a doctor's ability after meeting him or her.

It is important not to judge the competence of doctors by the size and colors of their advertisements or the beauty of their offices. Most doctors in the United States are members of the American Medical Association (AMA); this is merely a trade association, not a licensing agency. Doctors in the United States are "peer reviewed." This means that they certify each other's competence. In practice, this leads to a situation in which the buyer must beware. State licensing boards exist, but because they are composed of other physicians, their record of responding to judgments and even convictions for malpractice is poor. A doctor does not have to be board certified to advertise a particular type of medical specialty; it is a good thing for you to ask about, however, even if the answer will only tell you whether the doctor took an extra test. If the doctor did take an extra test, it may have been many years ago; the answer will not tell you whether the doctor is still competent.

Some doctors practice at teaching hospitals, publicly available, tax-supported institutions where new doctors are trained. This indicates a little more current knowledge and also that the doctor is respected in the old sense of having a "calling" to medicine. Faculty members at teaching hospitals tend to have excellent qualifications, can usually be consulted privately, and will give you their informed medical opinion, regardless, sometimes, of your ability to pay, especially if your condition is medically unusual. However, you have a right to be informed if an experimental treatment is planned and if there are any possible side effects.

"Internal medicine" specialists diagnose and treat illnesses of the internal organs. Specialists also exist for women's diseases, diseases of the heart, skin, bones, eyes, liver and kidney, ear, nose and throat problems, and just about any other disease the human body can develop. *If* you are confident that you know which specialist to see, call the specialist clinic directly; they sometimes take unreferred patients, depending on their specialty.

You might wish to consult a physician who practices a form of medicine that you are familiar with in your culture and is outside this country's tradition—for example, acupuncture or homeopathy. These medical treatments are legal in most states if performed by a licensed practitioner. Many people have gained great relief from their illnesses by using nontechnological medicine; we suggest that you ask the doctor's office for the name of someone you can call for a reference.

Besides doctors, there exists a whole class of so-called healers who, in fact, take money for fake or useless treatments. These people are called "quacks." (Quacks are named for the Dutch word, *kwakzalver*, which means charlatan or deceiver.) If "quackery" can be proven, the individual may be prosecuted and sent to jail after conviction.

DIAGNOSTIC TESTS

To diagnose your illness, the doctor may order "tests." There are two meanings for this word, which often confuses newcomers. These are *not* tests such as those you take in school, which you must "pass" or try to do well in. These are medical diagnostic tools that tell the doctor what is wrong with you. Thus, a doctor who orders an eye test, for example, is asking the laboratory to check your eyesight and determine whether you need glasses. Occasionally, someone tries to memorize the eye chart to do well on the test. This defeats its purpose. If you need glasses, the eye test will help the doctor decide what kind of glasses to prescribe. If you memorize the chart, the doctor will not know how to help you.

Be sure that you understand the process of a test or examination ordered or performed by a doctor, so that you can decide if you wish to submit to the procedure; often there are alternative tests that a doctor can order to achieve the same results. For instance, if you are female and a vaginal examination is proposed, and you are from a culture where an intact hymen has cultural significance, make sure that the doctor understands your concern before you submit to the procedure.

Your doctor should be working in your best interests. Ownership of laboratories and hospitals by insurance companies or large corporations may cause a doctor to forget this. Knowing of such connections can help you differentiate between a physician's concern for your well-being and meeting a target number of diagnostic tests or hospitalizations for the month. Do not let a doctor schedule a test for you without understanding why you need it. And to control your costs, verify that a test is not being duplicated; ask if a previous test would give the same information. Ask to see copies of all tests for which you are billed.

CLINICS AND HOSPITALS

The most visible type of clinic is the walk-in clinic, usually located in commercial areas. Anyone can just walk in, register, and wait to see a licensed physician, whom you will pay through the clinic. Not all doctors are affiliated with hospitals or clinics, but most of the ones you will be seeing do have a clinic or hospital affiliation.

Hospitals have two types of clinics that treat emergency cases: a "first-aid" or walk-in type of clinic for minor emergencies and a true emergency clinic for things like heart attacks or gunshot wounds. Be careful which one you go to, since you can wait all day to see a doctor in the emergency ward, when what you really wanted was the walk-in clinic for a small problem.

If your illness requires hospitalization, your doctor will admit you to a hospital. The doctor may only be willing to send you to a hospital she or he is affiliated with, so if you are inquiring about medical care, always ask which hospital(s) your doctor is affiliated with and then check with knowledgeable people about its reputation.

If you need hospitalization, have no health insurance, and are unable to pay, you can go to a county hospital. These hospitals are obliged to treat anyone who shows up, regardless of ability to pay. In exchange for free treatment, you will be seen by "interns" and "residents." These people are doctors in training who are supervised by an attending physician. County hospitals are almost always understaffed, which means that you may have to spend many hours waiting for an appointment, but the care is usually first rate.

LIFE-THREATENING EMERGENCIES
American doctors do not make house calls. If you are experiencing a life-threatening medical emergency, dial 911 on your telephone, or if 911 service is not available in your area, call the telephone operator (press 0) to report the nature of the emergency. If you are a college or university student in a dorm, call your campus police or security center by dialing the university operator and describing the nature of the emergency. If you are not able to move, an ambulance will be sent to take you to the hospital.

Here are some situations that a large hospital in the Midwest considers severe enough to be treated first in its emergency room:

Severe difficulty breathing; foreign body lodged in trachea

Chest trauma (shock or injury) such as heart attack or gunshot or knife wound

Burns caused by fire or chemicals, to either eye or skin
Electrical burns
Heat exposure; temperature over 104 degrees F.
Cold exposure, "frostbite"
Body temperature less than 96 degrees F.
Near drowning
Overdose of sleeping pills
Any signs of paralysis
Drug overdose

As a general rule, Americans use hospital emergency rooms for immediate assistance for any situation involving trauma or bleeding. In this heterogeneous society, urban hospital emergency rooms have interpreters available for many different languages.

PAYING FOR MEDICAL CARE
Unlike many other countries, the United States does not have a tax-supported health care system. What you will find is a system involving private health insurance providers. Although any doctor who sees patients will send out a bill for services, if you have health insurance,

the money to pay the doctor does not come out of your pocket directly. Instead, medical costs are paid for by families, individuals, companies, and institutions that make small payments on a regular basis, weekly or monthly, into an insurance fund or pool. These funds pay the doctor or hospital for services the insurance company deems "covered." Health insurance coverage varies from Major Medical, payments to be made only for the most serious and life-threatening illnesses, to Complete, which can include new glasses, dental care, physical therapy, or any other medical care the insurance provider will include in the policy.

Many businesses are affiliated with insurance companies that have an agreement with a Health Maintenance Organization (HMO). These are clinics that include doctors representing every medical specialty as well as doctors practicing family medicine or general medicine. Members of an HMO are encouraged to visit their facilities for routine checkups, to take care of minor problems promptly, and to try to avoid major illness by good nutrition and body care. However, visits to any doctor other than one who practices for your HMO, or a specialist referred by an HMO doctor, are not covered. If you have a job that involves a lot of traveling, this may not be a desirable type of insurance.

Most universities require that international students get health insurance. Some students come to the United States with health insurance paid for by their sponsoring government, but most will subscribe to whatever health insurance system their university provides. Group health plans cost around $30 per month and usually cover hospitalization. (The average cost per hospital stay in 1988 was $4,207.) If you wish, you can sign up for a "deductible" policy, which means that you pay the first, say, $25, and the insurance company pays the rest. This is usually available to teaching and research assistants as part of normal university employee health insurance coverage. Sometimes, your sponsors can put you on their health insurance policy, and you can pay your sponsors for the difference between what they were paying without you and what they will be paying with you on their policy. Compare coverage and costs before you decide.

In families where one spouse is self-employed and one is employed by a business that offers health insurance benefits, it is almost always sound financial planning to include the self-employed spouse under the coverage of the employed spouse. When both are employed, compare the benefits of each policy before deciding.

Commercial health insurance sold through individual agents tends to be more expensive and gives you less coverage than university or employer-provided group health insurance. Large insurance companies such as Northwestern Mutual and Met-Life have policies available to visitors who apply within two weeks of arrival.

A good policy should provide coverage of more than 30 days in the hospital and should be based on actual hospital and doctor charges, not a prespecified amount per day that may be less than the actual costs. Try to get a policy that covers outpatient services with a low deductible. Ask about these things before signing up for a policy written by an unknown company and sold by an individual, even of your own ethnic group. Yes, this is a complex area of American life.

DENTAL CARE

You will see ads on television for products to clean dentures or to hold dentures in place, which may lead you to believe that most Americans have poorly fitting false teeth. Nothing could be farther from the truth. American dental care, including the fluoridation of water, has reduced tooth loss to a minimum. Children should brush their teeth with a toothbrush and fluoridated toothpaste at least twice a day. This practice allows them to avoid bad tooth "cavities" until they are 30 years old or older. "Flossing," or the use of thin strands of special dental tape between the teeth to remove food particles and plaque (material that coats teeth and causes food particles to stick) also helps keep teeth healthy. While adults may use a mouthwash to keep the mouth smelling fresh, brushing with toothpaste twice a day and flossing can allow you to keep your own teeth intact all your life.

If you should develop a toothache or a pain inside your mouth, make an appointment to see a dentist immediately. Since most people see dentists located in their residential neighborhood, ask some neighbors whom they use and how expensive that dentist is. Yellow Page listings, while available, cannot tell you how capable a person is, so it is better to ask someone.

Both men and women practice dentistry, so if you have a preference, you can choose whoever will make you feel most comfortable. Dentists, like other medical professionals, are licensed to practice by the state after a course of training that is the equivalent of that for a physician. Dentists are trained in special dental schools that often have "free" clinics. If you use a dental school clinic, you will find that the people who treat patients are dental interns or residents, acting under the supervision of an attending dentist, just like the doctors at a county hospital. You should have no hesitation in using a dental school clinic; the care will be fine.

Sometimes dental insurance can be included in your general health insurance; sometimes it must be obtained separately. If you do not believe you will need major dental care, you can choose not to take dental insurance and pay privately for whatever care you need, should the occasion arise.

THE DOCTOR-PATIENT RELATIONSHIP

The traditional practice of medicine in the United States is based on the assumption that the body is an object separate from the mind, a machine that, when it needs fixing, has to be sent to a doctor instead of a mechanic. The fixing usually involves pills or injections or some other chemical or surgery to make a patient well or at least take away any pain. The perspective is changing, albeit slowly, to the practice of slightly more holistic medical care, care that will treat the whole person rather than just the body.

In the meantime, however, this treatment of a sick person can be intimidating for a newcomer who has been used to more participative medical care. You do not have to be treated in any way that is demeaning to you, but you have to be willing to ask questions and require answers from your physician.

The relationship between doctors or other healers and their patients is one of great trust in America, as it is anywhere in the world. Historically, a doctor had a lot of power and status in this culture, and his (it was a male-dominated profession then) pronouncements were not questioned at all. A new concept, that of patient autonomy (patient's choice), has changed this. Now, the doctor is beginning to be viewed as a primary source of diagnosis and information about options. The patient, once advised of all alternatives, is the one with the authority to give informed consent to any procedure or treatment and the person responsible for the consequences of agreeing to any procedure, treatment, or waiver of rights. If you come from a culture of authority and obedience, this becomes rather annoying. You ask a doctor: What should I do? He responds: "Well, you could do x, you could do y, and you could do z. But it is your decision." If you are going to need medical care in the United States, it is important to understand that patient autonomy is an important way for you to stay in control in the midst of conflicting interests in the medical industry.

Patient Rights

There are many conflicting interests in the medical industry. You just want to get well. The doctor wants to be paid for services provided, the hospital or its controlling public corporation wants to make a certain profit per day per bed, and any insurance company involved does not want to pay a cent. So here are some rights you should keep in mind.

- You are in charge of your body.
- You have the right to be informed about your condition. If you do not understand what you are being told, you have the right to ask for a translator or a person who knows how to explain complex medical terms to the lay person. You have the right to use the facilities of a medical library to find out more about your condition.
- You have the right to ask how much a particular test or medical procedure will cost.

- You have the right to refuse treatment to the extent permitted by the law in your state and to be informed of the medical consequences of your actions.
- You have the right to choose to have an abortion subject to the laws of your state.
- You have the right to a "second opinion," to consult with another physician about your condition, at any time, without informing either doctor of the other's opinion.
- You have the right to see and copy your medical records.
- You have the right to walk out of the hospital "against medical advice" if you so decide.
- You do not have to pay for tests or treatments that you did not consent to.
- You have the right to be informed of any continuing care requirements following your discharge from the hospital. What you do not have the right to do is sue a physician or other medical professional for malpractice if you do not take his or her advice and you get sicker.

Newcomers from countries where illness is a time for expressing family solidarity, care, and concern should not be intimidated by a doctor's private examination room or hospital rules on visiting hours. If you prefer that a member of your family be present or consulted, you should say so. If you would feel more comfortable in a hospital if you had a member of your family stay with you (one only, however), tell the doctors. If you would feel more comfortable if your baby were born at home, you can contact a midwife. There are almost always alternatives. As long as you understand the consequences of any decision you make, you can be in control of matching the alternatives to your cultural preferences.

Patient Responsibilities
While you have the rights described above, you also have certain obligations or responsibilities.

You have the responsibility to follow the treatment plan that you and your doctor have agreed on and to inform your hospital or doctor of anything you think they should know about your body or your health history, for instance, allergies and current medications. You must inform someone if you cannot follow an instruction, for either physical or cultural reasons. If you are not comfortable giving a specific reason, you can simply say it is personal. You are responsible for your actions if you refuse treatment.

You are responsible for paying for your health care either directly or through an insurance plan. If what the doctor or hospital charges is more than the amount budgeted by the insurance plan, you will be asked to pay the difference. You can ask to pay over a period of time, but it is your responsibility to ask.

Another kind of patient responsibility has to do with sexually transmitted diseases. If you contract a sexually transmitted disease in the United States (health tests prior to arrival screen out the likelihood that you contracted it in your home country), it is your responsibility to ensure that you do not spread it to others.

AIDS, which stands for acquired immune deficiency syndrome, is the popular name for an infection by the HIV virus that is invariably fatal; that is, you are almost guaranteed to die from this disease once it shows itself. It is transmitted primarily by sexual contact, heterosexual (between men and women) or homosexual (between partners of the same sex), or by sharing the infected needle of a drug user, or by receiving tainted blood in the course of a transfusion. Contrary to the propaganda of many countries, you *cannot* get AIDS by merely being in the same room with an infected American or any other person, by using the clothing or dishes of an infected person, or by hugging or kissing an infected person without any further sexual activity.

Sexually active people can partially protect themselves against AIDS and other sexually transmitted diseases, such as syphilis, gonorrhea, and herpes, by using a *latex* condom during intercourse. Given the proclivity of human beings to avoid planning in such situations, however, the better course of action is to refrain entirely unless you are convinced your partner is a thoroughly healthy and responsible individual.

LIVING WILLS
In case you or a relative are hospitalized for a very serious condition, you should know about a "living will."

This is a concept that is new to many Americans, not only to newcomers. A living will is a document that can specify your wishes in case you have an accident or some incapacitating terminal illness, asking that no "heroic methods" of modern technology be used to keep you alive, that is, that you should not be kept alive by breathing and feeding machines long after any hope of recovery. A living will is important not only to carry out the wishes of the injured or sick person but also to reduce the financial burden on a family. The 1988 average daily room charge in a hospital in the United States was $586; keeping someone alive as long as technology will allow can bankrupt a family.

If you are female, a living will allows you to specify your desire in case you are pregnant: Should you be saved at the cost of the baby, or should the baby be saved? These are very personal and possibly religious decisions that you may not wish others to make on your behalf.

It may be useful to add a clause to your living will specifying that in case of accident or injury resulting in hospitalization in a state that does not recognize living wills, you be moved to your state of residence so that the provisions of your living will can be carried out. While this kind of transportation is expensive, it may be the only way your wishes can be carried out.

Some states recognize living wills, others recognize a "power of attorney for health care" document, and some recognize both. A power of attorney for health care is a document in which you appoint a person to decide all health matters for you in case you are incapacitated. States that allow such documents have legal forms that you can request from the Department of Health. These forms present the options that are legal in the state. Some of the living will forms offered by a state's Department of Health or Health and Social Services indicate that your signature on the document certifies that you wish *to be* resuscitated or *to be* kept alive at all costs. Read the form carefully! If you wish stronger actions than those allowed in the standard form, you will need to contact an attorney who specializes in estate law (wills).

12 Managing Your Money

In America, financial responsibility is expected of both men and women. In many states, when a marriage is ended, marital property laws divide in half all assets *and* liability for debts of a couple. Whether working outside the home or not, women should be involved in financial decisions and know the family's means and its debts at all times.

Some newcomers to America arrive with a large amount of money and others with very little, especially once the home currency is translated into dollars. Even if you do not have a lot of money, however, it is good to know a little about the banking industry and how money flows through this economy.

The 14,000 banks that comprise the banking industry in America are not owned by the government, as is the case in many countries, although it is regulated by the government through the Federal Reserve System. The U.S. government guarantees that if a federally insured bank fails, everyone who deposited money in it will be reimbursed, to an upper limit of $100,000 (as of 1991). This is why it is preferable to trust your money to a financial institution that states it is a "Member FDIC," that is, a member of the Federal Deposit Insurance Corporation. If you bring savings worth more than $100,000 into America, you would do well not to entrust all your money to one institution but to open up several accounts, each at a separate FDIC-insured location.

FINANCIAL INSTITUTIONS

Financial institutions in America are of three basic kinds, although you cannot always tell by looking which type you are dealing with.

Banks are primarily designed to handle commercial and private checking accounts, make business and consumer loans, and provide "safe deposit" boxes, where valuables may be stored. Banks are commercial, or "for-profit," institutions.

"Savings and loans" (S&Ls) or "thrift institutions" take deposits from anyone and lend money primarily to people buying homes. The S&L uses the house as collateral or security, so that it can be sure of getting its money back in some way even if borrowers stop paying on the loan. These are also for-profit institutions. Savings and loans were originally designed to allow people to open savings accounts to save money for the purpose of buying their own home. After a "down payment" amount was saved, the bank would loan the rest of the money to make the house purchase, holding the "mortgage" on the house as collateral, so people could pay for their home as they lived in it.

"Credit unions" were created so that workers and government employees could pool their resources to provide loans to buy expensive items, such as automobiles, over a period of several years at lower interest rates than those charged by banks or savings and loan institutions. Credit unions are usually set up by large government or private employers as a benefit to their employees. In some credit unions, only those employees can deposit money or get loans. These institutions are not-for-profit.

Today, these three types of financial institutions are virtually indistinguishable from one another. They all want you to deposit your money in their care. What they are interested in is the use of your money for as long as possible; you should be interested in getting the highest interest rate for the use of your money. Choose an institution with the least restrictions on withdrawal so you can withdraw your money when you need it.

MONEY ORDERS AND CHECK CASHING

If you do not have a bank account that allows you to write checks, a money order is the safest way to send money through the mail, to pay bills, for example. *Never* send cash through the mail, as it can easily be lost or stolen. You can purchase a money order at your local post office and at some supermarkets and convenience stores.

There are check-cashing businesses in every city (look in the Yellow Pages for your city) where you can cash an employer's payroll check and buy money orders to pay your monthly living expenses. Compare the service fees per transaction that you would pay over a period of time to the service charges you would incur by opening a bank account. A check-cashing place is an excellent alternative for people on the move. Some newcomers are better able to budget their finances by using check-cashing businesses.

At most check-cashing places, you pay a fee of 1 or 2 percent of the transaction value. For instance, if you purchase a money order to pay your telephone bill for the amount of $35, you might pay an additional $.70 to the check-cashing establishment, bringing your total to $35.70.

In some cities, check-cashing places sell bus passes, subway tickets, and stamps. They may provide cash advances for credit cards, fax services, answering services, and photocopy facilities. You may also be able to wire money to family and friends within the U.S.A. from one of these businesses.

OVERSEAS MONEY TRANSFERS

You may need to receive money transferred to you from your home country. The transfer will be electronic, to your U.S. financial institution or its correspondent bank. If the money does not arrive within a reasonable period of time, you can ask the financial institution in the United States to "put a trace on the money." They will expect you to know the address of the bank from which the money was originally transmitted, the date of the transfer, the amount, and the transaction number that the originating bank supplied to the person who requested it. Often, the transaction has to pass through so many institutions electronically on the way to the United States that you may be surprised to find that a bank on the other side of the country had the last record of your transaction. As long as you have the originating bank information, you need not worry; your money can be found.

Banks, savings and loans, and credit unions in this country can honor checks drawn on foreign banks, since banks are connected by computer networks. The amount each institution charges for processing this kind of check varies, however, and it would be well to shop around for the best rate. In case a transfer of money drawn on a foreign bank is delayed, you may be able to negotiate a cash advance for some of the funds. However, you will pay interest on this advance payment.

To avoid problems, many people send money home by way of a friend. While this may be satisfactory for a while, you may eventually decide that you need a normal international transfer technique to move money back home. There are several ways to send money out of the United States. American Express offices in all major cities will send international money orders, as will all U.S. Post Offices. Check exchange rates to make sure you are getting the best rate possible. Large banks that have international banking departments can transfer money either electronically or by money order, but savings and loans and credit unions do not usually have that ability.

OPENING AN ACCOUNT

You do not have to be a U.S. citizen to open an account at a financial institution, but the institution will want some proof that you have enough money to make it profitable for them to do business with you. If you are a foreign student, you have already had to prove financial viability before you were allowed to enter the country, and your university identification card is often sufficient evidence. If you are transferring a large sum from another country, the institution may be all too willing for you to open an account, even if only temporarily. Do not be surprised, however, to find that a transfer has been reported to the federal government. Financial institutions are legally responsible for reporting any transfer of $10,000 or more. This is an attempt by the government to identify people who may be "laundering" money, that is, moving money made illegally into legal channels. Unfortunately, the reporting requirement and any possible subsequent investigation can catch newcomers unaware.

A financial institution will usually offer you two types of accounts into which you can deposit your money. Sometimes they have fancy and different names, but more often than not, they are called "checking accounts" and "savings accounts."

Checking accounts are accounts into which you deposit income and then write checks (cheques) against that deposit. You are asking the bank to act as a safe place for your cash, and you want to be able to take your money out with no penalty, when you want. The bank cannot use your money to make loans, since they do not know when you are going to need it. So they charge you for safekeeping instead of paying you interest. Checking charges vary. Some institutions charge on the basis of the number of checks you write per month; others charge a fee whenever your account balance falls below a certain amount. Other options include checking accounts that offer a low interest percentage as long as you maintain a minimum balance and charge you if the balance falls below it. Here is where the difference between checking and savings accounts begins to blur; some banks refer to this type of account as a savings account.

A savings account is an account into which you deposit more money than you take out over the long term. If you open a savings account at a bank, you are telling the bank that they have the use of your money for a longer period of time than if you were opening a checking account. Some banks will charge you for withdrawals over a specified minimum. Interest rates on savings accounts are higher than those on checking accounts.

Middle-income Americans generally have one checking account and one savings account and try to transfer a budgeted amount from checking to savings each month. If you are an employee of a large company, your employer may prefer to make a direct electronic deposit into your checking account on payday, instead of spending their money on printing and mailing payroll checks. You can then rely on getting your pay when it is due, and you can ask the bank to set up an automatic deduction to transfer a fixed amount of money from your checking account to your savings every month, if you wish.

When a financial institution advertises "free checking," it does not mean that printed checks are included, only that there are no charges for writing checks against your account. Personalizing your checks with your name is considered an additional service, and a service charge for printing the checks will be deducted from your account. When you open a checking account, the bank personnel may show you a selection of print styles for checks—some colored, some ornate, and some plain. You do not have to have a fancy design for your checks to be accepted at a store or by your bank. All that is required is money in your account to cover the check.

Financial institutions sometimes offer investment advice to those who are in the upper income brackets, whereas a bank's financial advisor is an expert on various types of savings instruments offered by that bank, such as Certificates of Deposit (CDs). If you need advice on bettering your financial situation, consult a career and vocational counselor.

WRITING CHECKS

A sample of a completed personal check is shown below. Unlike banking practices in Commonwealth countries, you have no means of controlling the ultimate disposition of your check. Writing "For Payee Only" or "For Deposit Only" on the front of the check has no effect. Disposition is the payee's decision.

When you receive a check where you are the payee and you wish to deposit it, you have to tell the bank who you are and what your account number is. Fill out a deposit slip from the back of your check book, turn the check over, and write at the top of the space provided for endorsement, "For Deposit Only." Sign your name below that line as it appears on the front of the check. If you forget to add these words, the check can be cashed by anyone—it is assumed you have "endorsed" the check—giving your right to the money to the person holding that piece of paper (the bearer of the check).

```
┌─────────────────────────────────────────────────────┐
│ John Doe                        CHECK # # # #       │
│ 111 Any Street #1234                                │
│ Any Town, WI  53151-1502       Month/ Day/ 19XX     │
│                                                     │
│ Pay to the Order of: Hunt Apartment Managing Co. │$211.25│
│                                                     │
│ The Sum of:   Two Hundred Eleven and 25/100 ——  Dollars│
│                                                     │
│                                                     │
│                              Your Signature         │
│                              ─────────────────      │
└─────────────────────────────────────────────────────┘
```

A personal check

If you wish to cash a check made out to you, instead of depositing it in your account, you will probably need some identification to show the bank teller. If you cannot find a bank willing to cash a check made out to you, you may have to use a commercial check-cashing service.

Checks drawn on a bank in a different state or country take between 2 and 14 days to "clear" (process) so that your account is credited with the money and you can withdraw it. This is one reason it is better to carry traveler's checks or a cash withdrawal plastic card if you plan to cross state and national boundaries.

Never give your checking account number to anyone, especially not to anyone offering a credit card over the telephone, to anyone offering a "prize," or anyone who claims to be a representative of a bank or the government doing some "checking up" on possible problems. These are all "scams," dishonest techniques to part you from your money. Official notices will come directly from the bank or an official agency in writing and by mail, on letterhead paper. If you are suspicious, call the telephone number on the letter to confirm that it is official business before doing anything at all.

KEEPING RECORDS

It is your money. You should know what amounts you received or started from and how much you spent and where. Keeping a check register and writing down the payee and amount of each check is essential.

The bank sends you a statement at the end of the month giving its version of deposits, checks, and charges against your account. It is then your responsibility to match your records with the bank's and to notify them of any discrepancy. This is called "reconciliation." The bank expects you to do this; most even provide a reconciliation worksheet on the back of the statement for you to follow. The fact that your monthly statement is generated by computer does not make it accurate. Human error is most common during data entry, and deposits made by mail can go astray.

DEBIT CARDS AND AUTOMATED TELLER MACHINES

When you open an account, the bank officer may ask if you would like a card that can be used in a cash-dispensing "automated teller machine" (ATM). This plastic card with a magnetic stripe on the back, known as an ATM card or a debit card, can be used to make withdrawals, deposits, transfers, and inquiries to your account at an ATM that is connected to your bank's electronic network. You can sometimes use your debit card to make purchases without your having to write a check if your bank and the merchant you wish to purchase from have the appropriate computer setup. Your card number enables the bank to transfer money to the merchant from your checking account for the amount of your purchase, electronically.

Most banks in the country own one or more automated teller machines and make agreements with other banks to share machines. If you get a debit card, it can be used with any machine that displays the same picture ("logo") as any of the pictures that are on the back of your card. If you say you want a debit card, the bank may mail you a card and a "personal identification number" (PIN) that is your electronic signature or may ask you to choose a PIN yourself at a machine in the bank. You must keep this PIN a secret. *Do not* write it on the card.

Each ATM model has a different way for you to ask for and receive your money. When you ask a machine for

At an automated teller machine (Photo by Shauna Singh Baldwin)

money, the request is sent electronically from the machine, through the electronic network using telephone lines, to your bank. Your bank's computer then tells the machine whether you have enough money in your account, and the result is that the machine either gives you the money or not. When you receive money, that money has come from your account and is no longer available to cover any checks you may have written. The deduction is immediate. If you are not sure how to use an automated teller machine, ask the bank officer to show you. You may not want to use a human teller again.

A financial institution's responsibility to you is to keep your money safe, to give you the services it contracted to provide, to report your transactions accurately on your statement, and to give you your money back if you request it.

Your responsibility to the bank is simple: do not write checks asking the bank to pay people if you do not have enough money in your account. Sometimes this happens inadvertently. If it happens often, your bank—and the person to whom you wrote the check—will become less and less forgiving. Most businesses will charge you money, usually $10 or $15, if a check you wrote to them comes back from the bank with a notation that there are "insufficient funds" to cover the amount on the check. The bank will charge you as well. If this happens too often, however, you can be charged with criminal intent to commit fraud.

CREDIT CARDS AND BORROWING

A credit card is a plastic card that you can present at a store to pay for your purchases. The money for the purchases is paid to the merchant by the credit card issuing bank. For your part, you agree to pay the credit card bank the amount of any purchase you have made, plus interest on the outstanding amount, once a month. You have use of the credit card bank's money all month long, subject to a maximum limit, as long as you make the minimum monthly payment and are willing to accumulate a liability for interest until the balance due is paid off. The interest charges on credit cards are high—between 15 and 21 percent. To avoid all interest charges, pay each bill in full as it arrives.

Credit bureaus are notified when someone fails to pay a telephone company, store, or doctor, and agencies marketing credit cards or loans rely on their information. This is not always fair or accurate information, but it is the norm in use to establish whether a person is a good credit risk. Financial institutions are quick to offer credit cards, as long as there are no negative credit reports about you.

When you first enter the United States, you are unlikely to be considered a good credit risk even if you have records to prove your credit worthiness in your home country. Once you have enough money for the down payment on a car or a house, and a job to help you sustain payments, you will probably be able to get a car or home loan. For the short term, then, your only resource if you need to borrow money is likely to be a personal loan.

Most newcomers have friends from the old country or a sponsor from whom they can borrow. Newcomers used to verbal agreements in their home countries may be surprised when a lender asks for their signature on a "personal note" if the loan involves hundreds or thousands of dollars. This is a common practice and acts as a record of the loan, any collateral, and payment schedule. It does not necessarily indicate any lack of trust in your willingness to return the money.

The lender can also ask for security for a loan, so that the personal note is a "personal secured note." The common security offered by newcomers is jewelry. Be prepared, however, for this to be rejected. People in countries that have known great instability value gold and jewelry. America has not had a war on its soil since the latter half of the nineteenth century, so jewelry is often considered ornamentation, not investment. A better security may be to offer to work to pay off a personal loan; this is called "working out a trade." To protect yourself in such an agreement, you need to set a value on your time—the legal minimum wage in America as of 1991 was $4.35 per hour—and then agree to a fixed number of hours you will provide to pay off the loan and over what period. If there are other family members with you, you might structure the agreement so that the loan trade-off can be performed by you and other signatories to the agreement. This sounds impolite and legalistic to people from many cultures of the world, but it is a vital part of protecting the freedom you have come to this country to enjoy.

TAXES

For each year you are resident in the United States, whether you are a citizen or not, you have to "file" (complete and send in) federal and state income tax returns. Form 1040 is the usual federal form, but there are others, and most states have state income taxes. You must report all your U.S. income for the calendar year (January 1 through December 31) by April 15 of the *following* year. Only if your country has no reciprocal tax agreement with the United States would you need to report your world income.

We mentioned that financial institutions have a responsibility to report large transactions to the government. They are also responsible for reporting to the Internal Revenue Service—the federal tax-collecting agency in America—how much interest you make from deposits in your checking and savings accounts. The amount you report on your tax return (completed tax form) should match the amount reported to you by the bank.

BUYING "ON TIME"

If someone approaches you with an offer that seems too good to be true, it probably is. Encyclopedia purchases, music and book clubs, "complete sets" of pots, pans, and plastic containers, and magazine subscriptions cause great anguish to newcomers who do not realize that you can say *no* to an unrequested item that appears in your mailbox after you have purchased the minimum you committed to. Before you request a complete set of a product, ask yourself if you *really* need the item, if you can afford the minimum purchases required by your initial commitment, and if you can get the same product for less money in a store.

Investigate carefully before you buy anything "on time," that is, with payments spread over many weeks, months, or years, because you will, in effect, be borrowing money to purchase the item. Not only can the interest total more than the worth of the item but you may be stuck with merchandise that does not live up to its claims. Because there are so many choices in America, you may be tempted to buy from people who seem to promise that you will find heaven on earth, become wealthy beyond your wildest dreams, or achieve your heart's desire if you will only buy and use their product or service. Our advice is: Resist temptation!

It is against the law for salespeople to promise something they have no intention of delivering. It also constitutes consumer fraud. "Bait and switch" is one type of fraudulent sales technique. In this type of "scam," or illegal sales technique, an expensive item is advertised or shown at a very low price. When you go to actually buy it, however, you are told the advertised item is out of stock and are then shown something inferior, usually at a higher price than you would normally pay for that product. If someone tries this, refuse to do business with that company, tell your friends not to do business with that company, and report the company to your local consumer fraud office, or Better Business Bureau.

You usually have 48 hours to change your mind about buying anything on time. If you sign a sales contract and then decide you do not want the item, you must return it within 48 hours, or the contract remains valid and you will have to pay whether you want the item or not.

GAMBLING, LOTTERIES, SWEEPSTAKES

In America, games of chance include cards, dominoes, bingo, and dice; betting at dog or horse races; and buying a lottery ticket. Gambling will enable you to win money rather than lose it only if there is some sort of skill involved, and the money you can gain is in proportion to the amount of skill you *actually* have rather than the amount of skill you *think* you have. In some states buying a chance at a prize—for instance, playing the state lottery—is allowed, but playing games of chance for money is illegal. In others, both are legal. Check before you play.

If all you are looking for is entertainment, gambling no more than the cost of an evening out on the town is fine. But gambling can become an addiction, so be aware of how much you are spending in relation to your other financial responsibilities.

LIFE INSURANCE

The insurance industry in the United States is a form of legitimate gambling. When you buy life insurance, you are really buying a bet on how long you will live. The purpose of insurance is to protect your family from having no money after you are dead, either to pay burial costs or to support your survivors if you are the main wage earner. The insurance company is betting that you will live a long time. The insurance company calculates whether you are a safe bet by considering factors such as your age, your health, your habits, your gender, and your family history. If you are a safe bet, they will agree to sell you life insurance, and you agree in return to give them a sum of money each year, known as a "premium." When you buy life insurance, you specify to whom the benefits should be given when you die. And every year as you renew your policy, the life insurance agent gets a commission on the sale. This is why there are so many life insurance agents in the United States.

Life insurance for a newcomer is necessary only if you have dependents for whom you are the sole breadwinner or if you have debts (such as a mortgage) that you would like paid in full if you should die. If you commit suicide, the insurance company does not have to pay any money to your beneficiaries. You can designate an overseas beneficiary of your life insurance when you buy it; however, it is best to state the amount of the payout expected and the names and addresses of the beneficiaries in a will.

WILLS

Living wills are discussed in Chapter 11. An estate "will" is a legal instrument that describes your wishes for the distribution of your assets when you die. If you are a resident of the United States and you die without a will, your estate will be handled by the government, which most often means that it will be divided equally among your heirs—male and female. Check the laws in the state where you live, however. If you have any property that you wish returned to relatives in the old country, you should have a will that specifies these wishes. You can make your own will by filling out a legal form available from any state legal aid society. You do not need a lawyer unless you wish to do more than simply write down who should get what and appoint a person to act as your executor, the person who carries out your wishes.

CHARITY

Not everyone in the United States is well off. There are those who have no place to live except in a cardboard box or an automobile. They are called the "homeless," and their plight is real. You will see street people who may be mentally ill yet refuse to live in an institution; they are free to live outside if they are judged harmless to themselves or others. There are others who are unable to receive care because of lack of facilities and government funding.

The poverty line in 1991 U.S. dollars was $12,000 per year for a family of four. If you come from a country where the poverty line is much lower, you may consider this amount excessive. However, $12,000 per year does not go far in a large city in America even for a single person. This is not a country in which it is considered simply bad luck to be poor; sometimes it is considered the fault of the unfortunate, the assumption being that the poor person must not be working hard enough. This attitude stems from a basic belief that if you show your willingness to work, someone will give you a job. Sometimes this is, indeed, the case, but economic conditions and discrimination in employment can make jobs scarce for many willing workers.

At one time, in the 1960s, middle-class youths, "counter-culture hippies," roamed the streets begging passers-by for "loose change." Some of this 1960s behavior has remained as an artifact for teenagers during their rites of passage to adulthood. Refusing to give them money is not considered uncaring. Others requesting charity donations are dealt with as you see fit.

In many countries in the world, families take care of those who cannot take care of themselves. The chronically sick, the mentally ill, the old, and the handicapped are viewed far more kindly in America than anywhere else in the world, perhaps because they have fought for rights but also because this society, unlike many other cultures, does not view them as the cause of their sickness or pain. Nor is it considered a result of genetic inheritance or bad luck. It does view them as problems to be solved, however, and it does expect them to contribute as much as they can, in whatever way they can, to support themselves.

While there are many families in America who do take care of their own, sometimes family members cannot care for older, handicapped, or poorer relatives without financial assistance. Government and voluntary organizations can assist the individual (not the family) with housing and job information, training, and, as a last resort, temporary financial assistance. Taxes help pay for these social programs, but people give money, in addition, to charitable institutions.

Americans make a distinction between charity and "welfare." Many Americans believe that those who are able to work but receive government support (welfare) while in their peak earning years are doing something morally wrong. The value placed on hard work rests on the belief that hard work builds strength of character; thus, it is felt that any assistance to a person who does not really need it is a disservice to that person.

Charity is voluntary giving. Reasons for donating time and money vary; for example, religious belief, helping those who are going through hard times because the giver also experienced hard times, or simply helping those who are less well off than oneself.

If there is one value that most Americans (both men and women) feel strongly about, it is the fear of being indebted to anyone (including family members) or, worse, having to rely on the government for financial support. Because of American resistance to feeling indebted, you may find that what your culture may consider a friendship offering is viewed as a threat to the receiver's independence. Most voluntary organizations that help newcomers—such as International Institutes—concentrate on giving information, not money. Ethnic organizations may be more willing to provide financial assistance. Some voluntary organizations set up picnics, barbecues, and dinners for newcomers to meet Americans; others provide refugee and immigrant representation. It is advisable to ask about the purpose and objectives of an organization and the purpose of the event before attending, even if it is free. The Appendix provides a list of voluntary agencies in the major cities of America.

While Americans often give enthusiastically, their common expectation is that charity is a short-term solution to your situation. What many cultures consider mere hospitality is likely to be viewed in America as charity. People will expect you to share expenses or work off any obligation to them as soon as possible, feeling sure that you will not want to feel indebted to anyone longer than necessary. Sponsors of new immigrants usually have plans for work that you can do for them around the house or in their businesses well before you arrive, so you will be able to earn your keep as soon as possible. Even if the work they find for you is menial in contrast to your qualifications and status in the old country, you are expected to be grateful for the opportunity and use it as a stepping-stone to better yourself as soon as possible.

One of the most valued commodities that people can give you in this culture is their time—whether to listen to you, drive you to an appointment, or even advise you. If you come from a culture where time is less important, it may be hard to understand why, say, an immigration lawyer may charge you $50 or more per hour just to talk with you. Remember that even advice in America is not free; and anyone who gives you free legal or job advice is performing a charitable service.

The expression of gratitude is expected to take the form of action to improve your situation as soon as possible, so you will not need assistance again. If you need assistance, accept it from voluntary agencies set up for this purpose or from people of your own culture, so that misunderstandings are less likely. You will be expected to pay back any money you borrow, even a small amount.

Newcomers from cultures where there is a vast difference from others in dress and behavior of beggars can find themselves offering hospitality to people who may in fact need charity or psychiatric care. Signs of prosperity are more apt to be thinness than fatness in this weight-conscious culture—and cleanliness. While offering either hospitality or charity is a value we hope you will retain, be careful of inviting strangers into your home, even if they show great curiosity about your culture, religion, or living quarters.

Providing shelter, hospitality, and guidance to friends and relatives from the old country is an excellent way to continue tradition and ensure that you maintain contact with your culture. Nevertheless, do not let yourself be taken advantage of, especially before you have found yourself a job or trade. For instance, visitors from home should spend their own money if you let them stay with you. Sharing all that you have before you understand the amount of effort it takes to earn it in this economy can lead you into needless debt.

As you move up the income scale in America, into more prestigious neighborhoods, or if you start your own business, you will get telephone calls and letters from many charitable organizations or their "telemarketing" companies. Telemarketing companies take a percentage of the money you give them for the charity. Any charity you contribute to—including a religious organization—must be willing to provide you with a receipt for your contribution, so that you can claim the amount as a deduction from your taxable income for that year.

If you cannot give money, volunteer work is an excellent means of helping people while learning new skills. Volunteering is a strong American tradition. You can volunteer to help in a hospital, serve at a soup kitchen feeding the homeless, help in running a used-clothing store, or offer to teach a newcomer what you have learned about living in the United States. Local newspapers often print requests for volunteers. No matter how depressed you might be from loneliness in your first few months in America, remember that people who are worse off than you are could use some help. Volunteering is an excellent way to conquer isolation and to begin to care about people who live in America, not just people back home.

13 Social Customs and the Law

MEN AND WOMEN

To newcomers from more agrarian economies, it may appear that American women have decided to become men, giving up their obligation to play a respected and needed role in the family unit. To newcomers from industrialized countries, it may appear that American women have lost the grace and charm that are the hallmark of womanhood in those cultures. As you probe American culture more closely, however, we think you will find that, while a personality profile of the American woman is impossible, there are certain commonly held values that underlie the absence of behaviors you may be used to.

The high value placed on directness in this culture—also called "not playing games"—makes Americans look on the coquetry that is so strong a part of male-female interaction in other cultures as manipulation. In some cultures, for instance, the assumption is that when a woman says "no," she really means "maybe." In America, we recommend that male newcomers interpret it as follows: she means "*no.*"

The Hollywood image of highly autonomous, liberated American females is not the norm across the population; the assumption of equality between the sexes has only recently pervaded American male-female relationships. The assumption of equality between the sexes means that males are expected to do work that would be considered effeminate in other cultures, such as cooking, washing the dishes, or changing a baby's diapers. This is an expectation that all American men do not yet share, and newcomers can sense this tension easily when it is unresolved in an American household. However, American men no longer treat women as fragile or unable to handle any task, however physical. In many households, American women are trying to raise children and hold full-time jobs, and you will find yourself impressed by their energy.

If you are a female newcomer from a country where women's rights have not been acknowledged either by the law or by the culture, or perhaps not to the same extent as in America, you may first feel a sense of euphoria at being treated as an equal and then some apprehension. Being equal to men involves the effort of becoming autonomous in decision making, being responsible for your own psychic and economic well-being. As you become used to equality of opportunity and being respected as an individual, it becomes harder to return to inequality. You need to ask yourself if the men in your life are willing to adjust to any behavior changes you decide to make.

There is strong antipathy—some of it grounded in Christian religious doctrine against homosexuality—toward any physical display of same-sex friendship in America. Men do not walk hand in hand here, and women generally do not touch except in greeting.

MARRIAGE

Since one of the delights of every family is to see its children married, marriage ceremonies in the United States can take on budget-breaking dimensions. While Americans who enjoy celebrations tend to celebrate marriages lavishly, a marriage in Las Vegas with recorded music by Elvis Presley and a five-minute service by a justice of the peace is just as legal. There is no upper legal age for marriage, so divorced people are just as likely to marry (for a second or third time) as are younger people.

Most Americans believe in romantic love, and everyone desires the perfect soulmate. Assisted and arranged marriages are viewed with suspicion, because they are considered to be imposed by external authority, rather than the individual's choice. Men and women meet one another independently—at school, at parties, at bars and nightclubs—and yes, through mutual friends and relatives. Virginity in males and females is not considered a prerequisite for marriage. Americans are getting married later in life than people in other countries, and some are choosing to remain single or childless. When they choose a potential marriage partner, most people restrict themselves to those eligible in terms of age, income, or ethnicity, but this is breaking down, and intermarriage across age, religious, ethnic, and color lines has become more common.

Citizenship is not required for obtaining a marriage license, nor is membership in a religious group. However, immigration laws can make your life very difficult if you decide to marry a U.S. citizen and you have not been granted permanent resident status. If you are not in the United States and decide to marry a U.S. citizen, the immigration laws say that the U.S. citizen must apply for a special visa for you called a "fiancé(e) visa." If a person who is not a U.S. citizen marries a U.S. citizen outside the United States, be prepared for the non-U.S. citizen spouse to wait up to six months outside the United States, until the immigration authorities grant temporary resident status.

The application review process is designed to exclude anyone who is marrying a U.S. citizen for the sole purpose of obtaining permanent resident status. You should be prepared for quite an intense scrutiny of your relationship by the FBI. If either party was married previously, the immigration authorities will require proof of termination of the previous marriage(s) by either death or divorce. If you are not currently in the United States and you wish to marry a U.S. citizen, you will be interviewed at the U.S. consulate in your country of citizenship, and your intended spouse will be interviewed separately at the closest immigration office. Once the application is granted and you enter the United States, you and your intended spouse have 90 days in which to be married, or the status "lapses" and you can be deported.

Every state has its own requirements for legal age of consent, but child marriages (either party below the age of 13) are not allowed anywhere in the United States, nor is any marriage legal without the consent of both the male *and* female involved, even if the parents of both parties agree to the marriage.

Many states have marital property laws that consider all property acquired or earned during the term of a marriage owned equally by both spouses. If you (or your spouse) wish to exclude certain property from this equal division in the event of divorce, you should consider having a lawyer prepare a "prenuptial," or premarital, agreement. While every state has its own set of requirements for obtaining a marriage license, all states require the couple to obtain a marriage license beforehand, whether the marriage is to be a religious ceremony, a civil ceremony, or both. In most states, but not all, the couple must also submit to a blood test for venereal disease and other medical conditions, such as rubella (German measles), before a marriage license can be issued. The blood test does not examine your genetic inheritance, nor is there any legal barrier to marriage between people of different races. "Miscegenation" laws, or laws barring marriage between people of different races, have been outlawed as unconstitutional since the 1960s.

Once you are married, you do not automatically obtain either permanent resident status or U.S. citizenship; you are granted temporary resident status for a two-year period. At the end of two years, you can be granted permanent residence if you can prove in yet another immigration interview that you are *still* married. This can be problematic, particularly if you do not have children as "proof" by that time. Joint ownership of assets such as a car or house does not prove that you are still married. Interestingly enough, the only true proof is joint ownership of liabilities.

DIVORCE

A couple is not considered legally divorced if they dissolve the marriage only in their home religion or ethnic tradition. Only divorces that have been obtained through the American or other civil legal system are considered legal. If a religious divorce is desired, that may be obtained in addition to the civil divorce, but the latter is mandatory. Annulment, or the "undoing" of a marriage that has never been consummated, is also acceptable as a legal dissolution but again, only if performed by a civil court.

Divorce in the United States is a state-by-state legal matter, with some states more lenient than others on grounds for divorce. The statistics on U.S. divorces are the indicator most used to decry the "breakup of the family in America." It is true that the divorce rate (one for every two marriages) is one of the highest in the world, and it is becoming accurate to say that many Americans practice serial monogamy. However, what is important to note is that socially, marriage is viewed in the United States as a contract for the maintenance and betterment of both parties. If one person is not performing his or her part of the contract, the other person has the option to declare the marriage void. Depending on the state, grounds for divorce include adultery, cruelty, desertion, alcoholism, impotency, nonsupport, insanity, bigamy, felony conviction, drug addiction, separation for two years or more except in cases of military service, and marriage under fraudulent conditions. Many states have now instituted "no-fault" divorce. In these divorces, no one has to show good cause for divorce; if one party wishes to dissolve the marriage, a divorce can be obtained. (Some states have provisions for counseling and a separation period.)

If you and your U.S. citizen spouse decide to divorce prior to the expiration of your two-year temporary residence visa and you desire to remain in the United States, we recommend that you be the petitioner for divorce, not your spouse. The unfortunate result of the 1986 immigration act has been that the U.S. citizen in a binational marriage has a great deal of power over the non-U.S. citizen spouse, and the incidence of domestic abuse and forced labor is a well-known outcome with no immediate solution.

BIRTH
Births must be recorded with the local government health department. A birth certificate with the child's name will then be issued to certify that the birth has been registered. The low rate of infant mortality in the

United States has led to the practice of naming the child immediately on birth. For those from cultures where it is not customary to name a child until a certain number of days after the birth, this can pose a dilemma. We advise you not to give the child a temporary name; the name on the birth certificate follows the child throughout life, and legal name changes are costly and time consuming. Many families give their child a family name and two sets of individual names—one traditional, one American. To find the meanings of English-language names, there are books full of names and their meanings which can be found in bookstores and libraries. Religious ceremonies connected with the birth of a child, such as male circumcision, may be held in the hospital or at a place of your choice; this is a matter for each family to decide.

A child born of foreign parents on U.S. soil automatically becomes an American citizen at birth. U.S. "soil" includes the forty-eight contiguous states, Alaska, Hawaii, Puerto Rico, the Virgin Islands, and Guam. The child may acquire dual citizenship if your country allows it. The United States will continue to count your child as a full citizen until he or she specifically renounces U.S. citizenship. Note that your American-born child may not petition for a change in visa status until she or he is 21 years old.

DEATH

Death certificates must be obtained from the appropriate local official, usually the county coroner, and signed by a licensed physician. There is no presumption of consent to donate internal organs in the United States; it is a matter of choice. You can indicate consent on the back of your driver's license. It is illegal everywhere in the United States to sell a body part for money. Most Americans do not understand that this makes it possible for people who have the money and power to procure body parts from countries of the world where it is not illegal. Since organs must be screened carefully for blood type and other physical conditions, most donations in the United States go through an organ donation "clearinghouse," where donor and donee are unknown to each other. Donations between family members are encouraged, as are donations of parts of a loved one so that another person's relative may live.

Burial or cremation and religious ceremonies attendant on them are considered a private affair under the First Amendment of the U.S. Constitution. Moving a body to another location, even to an overseas location, can be done. This must be accomplished by a licensed funeral director and is not covered by most health insurance policies. If you have to travel by air to attend a funeral, be sure to ask the airline for a "bereavement fare"; these are usually 50 percent off the no-advance-booking fare.

RELIGION IN AMERICAN LIFE

Many of the earliest European immigrants to the United States were fleeing religious persecution. When the states entered into "a more perfect union" and the U.S. Constitution was adopted, effective separation of "church" (meaning religion) and "state" (meaning government) was included as a clause in the first amendment. Religious freedom, the freedom to worship (or not) as you please, has been one of the hallmarks of American democracy and perhaps the one that will preserve democracy in this increasingly diverse nation.

In America, the term "secular society" is taken to mean a state that is worldly rather than spiritual. The separation of church and state removes any legal connection between organized religious bodies and government activities: for example, the president cannot be the head of any organized religion, the salaries of religious personnel cannot be subsidized by the government, and there cannot be religious political parties. In addition, it precludes any activity tending to foster official statements against religion. In that sense, the United States is a secular society, yet the president takes the Oath of Office with a hand on the Bible, and the Congress begins its day with a prayer. Businesses close on Christmas and Easter, which are Christian holidays, as do schools at all levels. However, civil marriages are commonplace; an employer is likely to grant a request for time off for a religious function if you offer to work overtime or on a holiday to "make up" the time; and formal prayers are not allowed in public school classrooms.

This separation of church and state has the effect of also separating the individual's spiritual and home life from work life to a greater extent than in cultures that do not value the independence of the state from religion. As a result of this, what you find in public life is the substitution of "ethics," a neutral concept of honesty and right and wrong, for "morality," which is considered to be a religious concept connected with one's home and spiritual life in the private sector.

Because of the separation of church and state, the official U.S. Census cannot ask about any religious affiliation. We must depend on religious organizations themselves to give us information about their membership. As a result, comparisons of membership statistics do not necessarily reveal which denominations have more adherents than another. As an overall guide to religious activity, however, the *1990 Yearbook of American and Canadian Churches* presents the following picture:

- About 60% of the total population consider themselves members of a religious group. Changing one's religion, called "conversion," occurs in about 0.5% of the adult population every year.
- There are over 340,000 houses of worship.
- Approximately 136,724,000 people consider themselves Christians: 79 million Protestants; 55 million Roman Catholic; the rest Old Catholic, Coptic, Greek Orthodox, Eastern Orthodox, and so on.
- Jewish organizations estimate that six million Jews live in the United States.
- Moslems estimate that there are 6 million members of Islam.
- Other religions, including Baha'i, Buddhist, Sikh, and Rastafarians, probably number less than 2 million.

Toleration of religious dissent is also an American hallmark. The Freedom from Religion Foundation estimates that 20 million atheists (people who do not believe in God) and agnostics (those who believe the existence of

God is beyond human comprehension) currently call America home. The United States is also the largest country in the world with a predominantly Protestant population.

Among Protestant groups in the United States, these ten are considered the most important denominations, or subsets, of Protestant Christianity (in alphabetical order): Baptist, Disciples of Christ, Episcopal, Lutheran, Methodist, Pentecostal, Presbyterian, Quaker, Seventh Day Adventist, and United Church of Christ.

Not quite as doctrine oriented as any of these ten denominations is a group that calls itself the Unitarians. Thomas Jefferson, one of the "founding fathers" of the country, is considered to have used his Unitarian beliefs as a basis for much of his writing.

If there is one difference between this religious heritage and others around the world, it is a concept that is so ingrained in American culture that it has the status of an ordinary everyday off-hand remark used to console those who believe they have been wronged: "Forgive and forget." Everyone accepts this as the way to behave. "Never forgive and never forget," which is normal in most of the rest of the world, is not acceptable to the majority of U.S. citizens.

While African-American communities tend to have their own mainstream religious organizations, such as the African Methodist Episcopal (AME) church, in many African-American and Hispanic communities "storefront" churches abound. A storefront church is one that holds its services in what used to be a commercial establishment. Preachers may be "ordained" (college-educated and certified to preach by an organized religious body) or not, as the congregation wishes.

One practice that churches of all these denominations have in common is that they hold scheduled services and are not 24-hour places of prayer. Many of them are closed between services or ceremonies and are not available as places of refuge, as are places of worship in other countries. However, American church congregations and Jewish synagogue groups have been active in reaching out to newcomers and funding voluntary organizations, English classes, adoption agencies, and in providing church or synagogue basements for prayer meetings for those of other faiths.

Native Americans or American Indians (both phrases refer to the same groups) have their own faiths. Their religious beliefs root them in the Earth as their Mother, giving the followers of these religions a desire to leave the Earth as they found it, devoid of man-made desecration.

New religious groups spring up all the time. "Mainline" religious groups, such as Protestants, Catholics, and Jews, have seen some new sects capture adherents by what they believe are less-than-honest techniques. These organizations, called "cults" by the press, have been accused of "brainwashing," or enticing people to join who are undergoing severe psychological problems and are in no position to judge whether or not the belief system they have been presented with "makes sense." The Rev. Sun Myung Moon's followers, of the Unification Church but popularly known as "Moonies," have been accused of cultlike activities, as have the followers of Dianetics and Eckankar.

People who have brought ancient religions with them, such as Buddhists, Hindus, Jews, Shintoists, Sikhs, and followers of Islam, Confucianism, and Tao, find themselves in a land where new faiths also find a home. If you follow any of these ancient faiths, you should expect to see some differences in the practice of your own rituals and customs by both Americans and immigrants who have been here for some time. Even the interpretation of the tenets of these religions can vary from what you are used to in the old country.

New faiths established in the United States, some of whom send missionaries outside the United States, include the Church of Jesus Christ of Latter-Day Saints, popularly called "Mormons," Jehovah's Witnesses, Christian Science, and the "fundamentalist" television evangelists who appear to be able to talk directly to you through your television set although they may be thousands of miles away.

Because of separation of church and state, all religious

organizations are sustained solely by member donations and are not state supported. If you donate money to any of these organizations, your donation is likely to be tax deductible as long as the organization gives you a receipt for your donation of money or for the value of anything you donate. The religious organization itself, however, is exempt from paying taxes on the money you donate.

As a foreigner, be prepared for missionaries to ask you about your religious background as they make you their target for conversion. You will not find them interested in your religion or denomination even while asking you to be curious about theirs. The American assumption of free choice is used to convince you that once you reach the age of majority, you need to evaluate and select a religion as an individual choice. The best defense against a too-enthusiastic missionary, one that still maintains politeness, is to state that you have freely chosen to follow your religion. Missionaries who go from door to door with religious materials are protected by the law. You have the right, however, to determine who they are before opening the door, to not open the door for them, and to tell them to move off your property. Noise pollution by blaring a loudspeaker with religious exhortations to passersby is punishable only by fines for noise; the content of the message may not be addressed by the authorities.

Religious Observance and the Law

The U.S. Supreme Court has decided many questions involving conflicts of rights in which religious freedom has come up against conflicting legal statutes. These decisions are usually accepted by all parties, but occasionally the problem persists. Public discussion of sensitive topics that divide religions cannot be prevented, but these discussions are usually handled with respect.

Sunday is considered the primary "day of rest" for religious reasons in every state of the United States. At one time, so-called Blue Laws prohibited commercial activity on Sunday, resulting in arrests for selling such things as toilet paper, for dispensing liquor, or for holding a public dance. This has not been the case for many years; most stores are open on Sundays, often 24 hours a day. There are still areas of the country and the economy where echoes of the older practice survive; for instance, all banks are closed on Sunday. If your primary day for religious observance is not Sunday, the Supreme Court has ruled, most recently in *TWA v. Hardison* (1977), that an employer may adopt any reasonable method of accommodation and insist that you accommodate yourself to that schedule.

Occasionally problems such as the question of abortion are carried into the streets. This issue is hotly debated in contemporary American politics and religion. Although 75 percent of the American public (1990) accepts the Supreme Court's "pro-choice" ruling on abortion—leaving the decision on whether or not to have an abortion to a woman and her doctor in the first three months of pregnancy—many people in the other 25 percent are not happy with that ruling. The latest ruling on abortion by the Supreme Court (1990) places the states in a position to pass their own more restrictive laws. Guam, Louisiana, and Pennsylvania now have passed laws that restrict the right to an abortion. Guam's law, for example, only allows an abortion to save the life of the mother and makes it illegal to tell anyone where or how to obtain an abortion. These state laws, however, are not yet enforceable, are in the appeal process and will eventually be heard by the Supreme Court, which will then be a position to either let the original *"Roe v. Wade"* ruling stand or overturn it to let the state laws become enforceable.

While the legal battle rages, street activism continues. People may legally picket in front of abortion clinics holding signs to protest what is going on inside, but if they lie down on the ground and refuse to move, or perform other behaviorally contraindicated acts, such as grabbing the arms of people trying to enter the clinics, they can and will be arrested. They then, as Henry Thoreau taught, must accept the consequences they incur as a result of having broken the law, including being fingerprinted, tried, and, if convicted, going to jail. What will happen in the future with the abortion issue is anybody's guess.

Some Illegal Practices

Since the Supreme Court is the final decision maker in matters involving the law and religious practice, the following practices are now against the law in the United States, even if your religion says they are holy or acceptable:

- possession of narcotics even if intended for use in a religious ceremony;
- bigamy (two wives) or polygamy (multiple-wife marriages);
- polyandry (multiple-husband marriages);
- carrying a gun or a knife of the size of a machete or a kirpan with you on an airplane;
- forcing a person to marry against their will;
- child (under 13 years of age) marriage;
- sacrificial or holy killing of any human being, child or adult. This is considered premeditated murder, a crime that incurs either life imprisonment or, in some states, the death penalty on conviction.

While animal sacrifice solely for religious reasons is not currently forbidden, health laws may be involved and animal rights activists may protest or picket. Most Americans consider animal sacrifice a "primitive and uncivilized activity, not suitable for rational, educated, human beings." The purpose of the sacrifice and the ownership of the animal may also be involved in the determination of whether or not this is considered an illegal activity. The Supreme Court is in the process of determining the legality of animal sacrifice as an integral part of religious worship in 1992. Local animal cruelty and health laws differ with regard to killing your own dog, cat, lamb, or goat, or biting a live chicken's neck; most Americans find this repugnant.

14 Safety and Dealing with Emergencies

Americans believe that anything short of tornadoes or earthquakes are emergencies that can be dealt with and survived. Though we cannot foresee every emergency that you may find yourself faced with, we deal with the major emergencies that anyone in America might face. We hope you will never need this information.

GETTING LOCKED OUT
If you find you have locked your keys inside your home and cannot get back inside, you will need to contact the building manager or owner or a locksmith.

If you find you have locked your keys inside your car you will need to find a phone and call the closest service station (if you are a member of a motor club such as AAA you would call their emergency number). Tell them the make, model, and year of your car. They will have to send someone out to open the door.

PLUMBING PROBLEMS
Plumbers are paid by the hour in the United States, are always busy when you have an emergency, and are expensive. There is usually a minimum charge per visit, even if they find nothing wrong.

If water does not flow at all from kitchen or bathroom faucets or flows with a brown color or strange smell, do not use it. Check with the Water Department in your area; the problem will probably be an areawide concern, and you will be told what to do.

If a toilet overflows, usually because you have attempted to flush too much down it, you will need to unblock it using a "plunger," a rubber suction cup with a long handle that is available at any grocery store, drugstore, or hardware store. Put on a pair of rubber gloves. Stand well away from the toilet, and place the suction cup over the hole of the toilet. Use the force of the suction to unblock the toilet. Remove the material causing the blockage and dispose of it in the trash. Flush the toilet. Mop up the water that overflowed. Spray the area with a disinfectant and an air freshener.

If a sink is blocked, use a long wire (unwind a coat hanger) to remove the strainer at the bottom of the sink basin. Sometimes you can scrape away the clogged material. If that does not work, pour some boiling water down the drain and use a plunger to compress the air in the sink. If that is unsuccessful, buy a commercial drain cleaning chemical at a grocery store—Drano is the best-known brand—and, protecting your hands by wearing rubber gloves, follow the directions on the can. As a last resort, call a plumber.

ELECTRICITY FAILURES

If the electricity fails, it may be because you have loaded too many appliances on one circuit. Remove the last one you plugged in and find the fuse box or circuit breaker in the house. In apartments, it is usually in the kitchen; in houses, it may be somewhere in the basement or outside the home. If you have a circuit breaker, find the switch that is in the "off" position and turn it on again. If you have a fuse box (it looks like a small cabinet with rows of small round fuses), put on rubber-soled shoes and gloves to be extra safe, and turn the main switch off before touching anything in the box. Find the fuse that looks burned out or that has popped out of its socket. A burned-out fuse will need to be replaced; the pop-out kind can simply be pressed back into place.

To replace a burned-out fuse, take the fuse with you to a hardware store and buy one exactly like it, that is, with the same number of "amps" marked on it. (You could cause a fire by replacing a fuse with one of higher amperage.) Replace the burned-out fuse with the new fuse and then turn the main power switch back on.

To find out if what is happening is an electric failure in the building or in the neighborhood, as after a severe storm or earthquake, rather than just in your living space, look outside to see if other people have lights on. If the street looks normal, check with your neighbors to see if it is a building problem. If it is neither a neighborhood nor a building problem, report the problem to your landlord or call an electrician.

HOME BURGLARIES

Most burglars are under the age of eighteen and are likely to wait for you to be out of your house before breaking in. Burglaries usually occur on weekdays between 10:00 a.m. and 2:00 p.m. when people are out at work. Burglars like to steal cash, small appliances, and anything that looks valuable—to them. One newcomer we know found that jewelry from her home country did not look valuable to her American burglar because of the difference in styling, design, and luster.

When you move into a new residence, ask the owner to change all locks and keys immediately. Most apartment and house front doors have wide-angle peepholes so you can check to see who is at the door before you open it. Use the peephole! Do not let anyone you do not know into your home unless you have seen proper identification. For instance, if someone at the door claims to be from the telephone, gas, or electric company, ask to see an identification card.

Do not identify your keys by attaching a name and address label to the keychain. If you lose your keys, change the locks. Even if you find your keys again, someone could have made copies of your keys in the interim.

Make your house appear occupied at all times. Even if you are trying to save money on electricity, turn on some lights when you leave for the day, and leave a radio on. Lock anything that can be locked, even if you are leaving the house only for a few minutes. Fix broken locks immediately. If you buy a telephone-answering machine, do not state your full name on your recorded message; just say what telephone number has been answered. If you do not have an answering machine, turn the volume of the telephone ringer down when you are away, so that neighbors cannot hear the continual ringing and know that you are gone. If you have to be away for a while, ask a friend or neighbor to collect your mail and newspapers, so that it will look as if you are still in town.

Do not hide valuables anywhere in the master bedroom, or in a desk, drawer, or closet. Burglars may be looking for drugs, so the medicine cabinet in the bathroom is not a good hiding place. Hiding valuables in packets of food, under laundry, behind heavy furniture, or in a built-in (not portable) safe is a better idea.

If you are at home when a burglar strikes, remember that your personal safety is more important than your possessions. Never try to confront a burglar; try to avoid contact. Lock yourself in one room and turn on the lights. If there is a telephone, call the police at 911, or dial 0 for the operator and ask for the police. Start making lots of noise. Sometimes this can frighten the burglar away; if not, it may draw the attention of your neighbors.

Get in the habit of being alert to any signs of forced entry. If there is a light on that you turned off or a window open that you had closed, do not enter the house. Someone might still be inside. Go to a neighbor's house and call the police. This is a point we should stress for newcomers from countries where calling the police would be like calling your enemy. The police in this country are there to help you in situations like this. Wait at the neighbor's house until the police arrive.

Give the police a detailed description of any items you find missing. The more information you can give them, the better. A list of your possessions with serial numbers and values for insurance purposes, or original invoices, may be helpful in recovering your valuables. And for future safety, ask the police to do a safety check of your premises and give you some advice on burglary prevention.

FIRE

If your living quarters do not already have a smoke alarm, buy one at the closest drugstore (they are quite inexpensive), install it in a central location, and keep it supplied with fresh batteries. The best alarms give warning "beeps" when their batteries are running low; if yours does not have this feature, test it once a month. Buy a small fire extinguisher for your kitchen, and read the directions so you know how to use it.

Use care in striking a match to the pilot light of your gas oven; gas can explode. Do not leave food cooking on the stove unattended. Do not use gasoline as a cleaning agent. Keep a large container of baking soda near the stove, to pour on top of a grease fire. Check the cords of your appliances from time to time to be sure they are not becoming hot, frayed, or smelling as if they are burning.

If you cannot quit smoking, be careful not to smoke in bed. Empty ashtrays in the toilet, not in a wastebasket.

Make a list of your personal possessions and the value of each. Maintain this list so you have a record of major additions to your possessions. Buy a fireproof safe for jewelry and valuable papers such as your passport and immigration papers and your diplomas and degree certificates. Buy fire and theft insurance sufficient to cover the complete loss of everything you own.

If you notice the smell of gas at any time, open a window in the kitchen, call your city's emergency telephone number for help (usually 911), and get out of the house. Do not try to fight a fire for more than 60 seconds. To prevent smoke inhalation, drop to your hands and knees, and crawl to the nearest exit. If you are in a tall building, do not take the elevator; use the stairs. Older buildings have fire escapes, steel staircases running down the outside of a building. Wrap a cloth around your hand before touching a door handle.

Do not try and save your possessions; save your life. If you are trapped by fire, try to stop smoke from entering by placing wet towels below each closed door. Place a wet towel over your nose and mouth and try to reach a window or door. Break the window with a chair or any other heavy object if you can and scream for help.

MEDICAL EMERGENCIES

Accidents in the home are the major reason for visits to a hospital emergency room. They can be prevented by immediately wiping up anything spilled on the floor, by not using small, loose rugs on a wood or tile floor, by not standing on chairs to reach high places (buy or borrow a step ladder), by not wearing garments with loose sleeves when cooking, by keeping matches out of the reach of children, and by making sure all candles are cold before you leave the house.

If you have a medical emergency, do not panic. The most important thing you can do is to keep your logical self in charge. Most cities have 911 service for emergencies. That is a telephone number that you can use any time of the day or night to reach emergency personnel, including medical personnel. It is to be used *only* for serious cases, but the care, given by people trained to respond to everything from childbirth to gunshot wounds, will be excellent. To get the emergency team to where it must go, first give the operator the address or the location of the emergency, then your name, and then what you believe the problem is. Do *not* hang up after giving this information; stay on the telephone until you are told to hang up or until help arrives.

If you are in an area that does not have 911 service, call your nearest fire department by dialing zero (0) for the telephone operator. While both fire and police department personnel are trained to respond to medical emergencies, American fire departments usually have trained emergency medical technicians (EMTs) available.

EMERGENCIES REQUIRING POLICE ASSISTANCE

The 911 system can also be used for *emergency* calls to the police in any situation involving the use of weapons, a robbery in progress, any threat to human life or imminent danger of great bodily harm including attempted suicide, a crime you are witnessing that is occurring at the time of the call or that has just occurred, major thefts or property damage of $1,500 or more, fire, or when in doubt about a major crime situation.

Police are dispatched to deal with emergencies in order of seriousness. Fire and ambulance are considered first priority with immediate dispatch. Situations involving life or death—suicides in progress, gas leaks, explosive devices, or robberies in progress—are next in priority, and the goal is usually to dispatch assistance within 5 minutes. Dispatch within 20 minutes is the usual goal for all situations that are less than life threatening, such as burglaries where the suspect is no longer on the scene or a fight. For minor injuries and property loss or damage that does not require immediate police attention, such as car theft or accidents without injury, the dispatch objective is 60 minutes. For all other complaints—for example, noise, landlord-tenant trouble, or animal bites—police would be dispatched as they become available.

In all other cases, dial the telephone operator (0) and say, "This is an emergency." Then give the operator your address and describe the problem as calmly as you can.

Assault in the Street

"Mugging" is the slang word for the use of force to remove your valuables when you are doing nothing but walking down the street. The legal term is "assault," and if you are injured during the assault, you can, in almost all states, receive help from the state Crime Victim Compensation Program. If you report the crime to a law enforcement agency within 5 days of the crime and file a claim within 1 year of the date of the crime, you may be eligible to receive medical care, paid hospital expenses, lost wages, mental health counseling, homemaker services, reasonable replacement costs of clothing and funeral expenses for a relative who has been killed as a result of a crime.

You cannot receive compensation from the Victim Compensation Program for the loss of the valuables taken from you. However, if you have insured your valuables and your insurance agent determines you are entitled to payment, your insurance policy may cover your loss.

People who are injured in automobile accidents caused by drunk drivers may also be eligible for Victim Compensation. Check with your state's Department of Justice or your local Crime Victim Compensation office.

Sexual Assault
Sexual assault is any physical sexual contact with a person without consent. In this country, sexual assault is a felony. In short, no one is allowed to have any sexual contact with another person against that person's will. In about a third of the sexual assault cases in the United States, the assailant is acquainted with the victim (hence the term "date rape"). If you are assaulted, report it immediately, no matter how you may feel. Dial 911 for an ambulance and assistance.

15 Difficult Situations

Here are some situations to which newcomers may find themselves uniquely vulnerable, and some guidelines for dealing with them.

IMMIGRATION QUESTIONING AND ARRESTS

Not everyone is comfortable with the number of people immigrating to this country. A book that clearly expresses this point of view is *The Immigration Time Bomb: The Fragmenting of America* by Richard D. Lamm and Gary Imhoff (E. P. Dutton, 1985). To quote an old American saying, "Forewarned is forearmed."

If you discover that you are the subject of an INS inquiry, you have certain rights. You have the right to remain silent if you are questioned by an INS agent or the police. You cannot be detained for refusing to answer questions or for the color of your skin. However, you can be detained if the immigration authorities believe you are illegally present in the United States.

If you are arrested, you have the right to remain silent and the right to consult a lawyer before you make any statements or sign any documents. You have the right to be released on bond and the right to a bond reduction hearing to lower your bond or obtain release without bond. You have the right to a hearing before you can be forced to leave the United States, and you must be allowed at least seven days to prepare for your hearing.

Immigration and Naturalization Service personnel may not search your home unless they have a search warrant, and you can ask them to produce this court order before you let them into your home. If you receive a letter asking you to report to an INS office, you should first seek advice from an immigration counselor at one of the voluntary agencies listed in the Appendix.

If you had problems with immigration at one time and

were able at a later date to obtain legal residency, you should know that prospective private employers are not allowed access to information in immigration records, but it may be available to other branches of government. Be careful about giving your Social Security number to government agencies, as it makes it possible for the agency to attempt computerized linkage.

CHILD ABUSE AND NEGLECT

American laws on child abuse and neglect are based on the premise that a child has rights independent of its parents. In other words, the authority of parents is limited by law. If the enforcement of parental authority —whether it is perceived as being for the good of the child or not—results in beating, injury, or sexual molestation of any child, it is considered child abuse. Doctors who suspect child abuse are obliged to report it to child welfare authorities. The penalty for child abuse or neglect is loss of custody of your children; your children can be taken away from you and placed in foster care.

We advise newcomers with children to observe and examine their behavior toward their children at all times. Loss of your family support network, plus economic and social pressure to survive in a new culture, can affect your behavior toward those you love without your being aware of it. Neglecting children's needs or burdening them with too much responsibility at a young age is a common problem in relocating families. Remember that they are adjusting to this new culture, too. They may seem to adjust faster, but you should not assume this or expect it of them.

You may be under pressure to maintain the illusion that you know exactly what to do under all these new circumstances in order to maintain your authority within the family. Ask yourself: Are you using words in a way you know will hurt or in a way that will support each family member? Are you resorting to violence to maintain your image? Do you call it "discipline"? If you find yourself lashing out at your children either verbally or physically, we urge you to get help. You can call one of over 1200 offices of Parents Anonymous or 1-800-421-0353.

Parents Anonymous is a support group for people whose isolation has led them to hurt—or may lead them to hurt—their children and who wish to stop. Parents Anonymous sometimes has support groups for people of a particular language or ethnic group as well. What seems to work best to control such behavior is to recognize it, to wish to change, and to share and communicate with others who have had similar experiences.

If you are not the abuser but wish to stop the abuse, ask a doctor, a social worker, a nurse, or a member of the clergy to help you intervene on behalf of your family. Look in the Yellow Pages for your local Child Protective Services, or simply call the operator and say you have an emergency.

WIFE BATTERING AND SEXUAL ASSAULT

It is tempting to believe that sexual abuse of a woman (or of a child) is done only by strangers. The truth is that the probability of abuse is greater within the family. Assertion of power by using sex is likeliest when a person's traditional role in a family is challenged. Recognize that your family will be reshaping itself. The relationships between males and females will have to be redefined in response to the economy in which you find yourself. Both men and women, not just women, should be expected to change. Realize that violence is not an acceptable response and that there are solutions, whether you are the victim or the batterer.

In many states it is considered rape if a man enforces conjugal rights without the consent of his wife. Such behavior is considered "cruelty" and is grounds for divorce in Alabama, Alaska, Arizona, Connecticut, Delaware, Georgia, Idaho, Illinois, Maine, Massachusetts, Mississippi, New Hampshire, New Jersey, New York, North Dakota, Ohio, Oklahoma, Pennsylvania, Rhode Island, South Carolina, South Dakota, Tennessee, Texas, Utah, Virginia, and West Virginia. This charge, however, is often hard to prove when it is only the wife's word against the husband's. For more up-to-date legal advice, consult your local Legal Aid Society.

You have many alternatives if you are abused in America. If you are female, there is no social stigma attached to living alone, even with your children, as in some countries. Moreover, women are able to work and support themselves here. You can demand your own respect, without requiring a man's protection. Call this toll-free number if you are abused and need help: 1-800-333-7233 (1-800-333-SAFE).

DRUGS AND ALCOHOL
Alcohol becomes the first resort as a stress-reducing agent for many newcomers to the United States because of its availability and cheapness in contrast to other countries. Watch yourself. How many drinks are you using to "relax a bit"? How many tranquilizers are you relying on to get to sleep at night? Have you started medicating yourself to "get going in the morning"? Are you giving the baby just a little more brandy to put it to sleep every night?

If you are watching a member of your family become addicted to alcohol or drugs, you will need to take care of your own needs and not allow the alcoholic to control your life. Do not enable them to drink or use drugs by overlooking it or making excuses for them. Remind yourself often that you are not the cause of your loved one's drug or alcohol addiction. Neither is the United States. Only the person using drugs or alcohol to cover up his or her own insecurities is responsible for his or her addiction.

Alcoholism and drug addiction are progressive diseases; this means they get worse as time goes on. The more isolated a person becomes, the easier it is for the disease to take hold. The way to stop the isolation is to get help from people who have lived through and continue to live with a drug addiction. Call your local chapter of Alcoholics Anonymous for help for the alcohol or drug user, or call 1-800-821-4357 (1-800-821-HELP) for hotline help. You can also call the local Al-Anon organization or 1-800-356-9996 (1-212-245-3151 in New York) to get help for the sober members of the family.

DEPRESSION

Depression does not usually hit newcomers until all one's food, clothing, and shelter needs are taken care of and the transition seems to have been made. The amount of time you plan to be separated from all that is familiar to you begins to insist on your attention. At that point, you may cease to find everything different enough to be interesting and start to find things different enough to be irritating. The greater the extent of the cultural differences between your home culture and America, the more apt you may be to become discouraged about your ability to adjust. Of course, every newcomer is not likely to become depressed. And every person's responses are different. How can you tell when slight discouragement has given way to depression that needs treatment?

Ask yourself these questions: Are you irritable? Are you forgetting simple things? Do you feel like sleeping all day long? Are you waking up tired? Are you unable to concentrate? Do you find yourself in tears over small matters? Do you trust your own driving? Have you lost interest in your work? Are you eating much more? Much less? Can you remember the last time you felt valuable? Have you had thoughts of suicide?

If your answers to these questions are significantly different from what your normal responses would be, and the situation is a persistent one, you have to ask for help. You need to call a doctor, a college counselor, or a friend. In America, there is a saying, "God helps those who help themselves." You must break the isolation that leads to depression in newcomers and seek help whether from a member of your own ethnic community or not. There is no shame in needing psychological help in this country; you will not be labeled "crazy."

OTHER PROBLEMS

"Hot Lines and Help Lines" is a Yellow Pages heading you can use to obtain help with any other problem. If there is no listing there, check with the 800 telephone information operator (1-800-555-1212) for 800 numbers you can call.

"Don't let anything get you down" and "Look beyond the obvious" are American sayings meaning think positive. No matter how many bad things happen, remember today is a new day, and to survive it, you must have faith that it will be better than yesterday. To this, we add some advice just for newcomers: try not to let the bad things that may happen to you color your thinking about America.

There is an old story we would like to share which makes our point. There were four people who went out drinking one night. One ordered scotch and soda, the second ordered rum and soda, the third ordered brandy and soda, and the fourth ordered vodka and soda. They all got very drunk. They all woke up with headaches the next morning. They all decided it was the soda that made them drunk. America is like that soda. It is going to be the backdrop for many good things that happen to you, but it is also going to be the most obvious common element of any bad things that happen to you. Look beyond the obvious, so that you do not behave like the four people in our story.

16 Beyond Survival

There is more to surviving in America than we have discussed here. After all, no book can prepare you for every circumstance you may find in this large and diverse country. After the practical details of living are arranged to your satisfaction, there is yet another decision to be made: Do you wish to stay monocultural (meaning that you operate in America without changing your behavior at all), or do you wish to begin the examination of American, old country, and personal values that is essential to becoming a bicultural or even a multicultural being?

Some newcomers to America can visit or live for years in expatriate communities without changing their values, customs, language, or behavior at all. Some become more aware of their home culture than they ever were at home—more aware even than family and friends they have left behind. They may send their children to school with Americans and run successful businesses in America but view American values with disdain or ambivalence. These are people who have decided not to change their perspective or point of view when exposed to another culture. Many newcomers have decided to return to their home countries with gladness and relief.

Their thinking might be like this: "I can function in America, but my own people understand me best, and I understand them. It seems to me that all the values my family and culture worked so hard to teach me are not valued here or are inappropriate in the situations I have faced. By learning American ways, I might find it hard to readjust to my home country's culture. And perhaps I do not really need to."

This is a valid attitude for people who plan to stay only a short time. However, while it is possible—indeed, necessary in your first months in America—to live in a cocoon of your own home culture, it is not good for your long-term mental survival. We know people who have lived in America as permanent residents for over twenty years but who decided to remain monocultural. They became tremendously successful in a monetary sense but now say, "Life in America has no meaning." The longer your stay, the more important it is to begin the process of becoming bicultural if you are to avoid this feeling.

Becoming bicultural is a slow progression through emotional stages as you adjust to your environment. At every stage you will be constantly challenged to make decisions that break old habits and customs and to acquire new ones.

Think of water. Imagine yourself as a molecule of water changing its form to adjust to a change in temperature. When its environment is really cold, water freezes, and we call it ice. When it can flow, we call it water. When it is hot enough, water boils, and as the heat increases, its molecules get more and more energy. Then we call it steam. Each different form—ice, water, steam—has different uses. It takes a lot of energy to make the transition from one form to another, but it has to happen if you are to adjust to your environment. Throughout, you are the same chemical substance, though called by a different name at every stage.

Successfully becoming bicultural is not only an emotional process but a reasoning process. A continuous one. It involves observing your own behavior and deciding which behaviors, reactions, attitudes, and values are based on your culture and which are your own personal ones. Similarly, it involves observing the people of the other culture and deciding (and asking, if necessary) whether the behaviors, reactions, and values they have are cultural or personal. It involves adjusting your expectations until they become more realistic in terms of what you are likely to find in this culture and overcoming the urge to withdraw. And throughout, there is the difficult but rewarding process of comparing both value systems, deciding which old country values you wish to keep and which American values you wish to absorb. The process will take much curiosity (a desire to ask questions and to listen to and understand the answers) and openness (deciding that you will assume that things *different* are not necessarily *wrong*).

America is an ongoing dialogue. You bring a new voice and a new point of view. With every newcomer, there is potential for less ignorance and more cultural exchange, less exclusion and more inclusion, less certainty and more listening. And even if you choose to try to challenge or change prevailing cultural attitudes, that, too, is part of American flexibility.

America is unique in the history of the world in that it offers the opportunity not just to follow "the American Dream" of financial self-sufficiency but also the opportunity to follow *your* dream. But you have to decide first: What is your dream? What sort of person do you wish to be in this country? Good luck, newcomer. May you find your dream. Welcome to the U.S.A!

Appendix

Information Sources

AUTHORITATIVE INFORMATION SOURCES
Newspapers
Los Angeles Times
New York Times
USA Today
Washington Post

National Television Network Sources
American Broadcasting Company (ABC)
Cable News Network (CNN)
Columbia Broadcasting System (CBS)
National Broadcasting Company (NBC)
Public Broadcasting System (PBS)

Radio Network Sources
AP Network News
American Public Radio Network
British Broadcasting Company (BBC World Network)
National Public Radio Network

Consult your local newspaper for ethnic television and radio programs.

Public libraries and their librarians can recommend further sources.

ENTERTAINMENT PRESENTED AS NEWS
Tabloid Newspapers
Star
National Enquirer

"Talk" Radio
Subjective opinions presented as the norm

Minimum Kitchen Equipment List

MINIMUM KITCHEN EQUIPMENT LIST	One Person	Two People	Two People & Child
Dinner plates	2	4	4
Soup/cereal bowls	2	4	5
Cups or mugs	2	4	4
Forks	2	4	4
Knives	2	4	4
Small spoons (teaspoons)	2	4	8
Tablespoons	2	4	4
Glasses	2	4	4
Large wooden or plastic stirring spoon	1	2	2
Slotted spoon	1	1	1
2-prong cooking fork	1	1	1
1 qt. saucepan	1	1	2
2 qt. saucepan with cover	1	2	2
Frying pans	1	2	2

In addition, you will need to purchase:
1 large sharp kitchen knife and cutting board
1 can opener
1 set of measuring spoons
1 or 2 mixing bowls
1 or 2 measuring cups (1 cup and 2 cup sizes)
1 strainer
1 dish pan to use in sink
1 dish drainer and/or rack
1 bottle of dishwashing liquid
1 package of sponges or reusable towels
1 plastic pot scrubber
1 dishwashing and vegetable cleaning brush
1 roll of disposable paper towels
1 large trash can (wastepaper basket)
1 roll of trash bags, generic brand
1 can cleaning powder (cleanser)
1 box presoaped "steel wool" pads
Kitchen towels
Oven mitts (gloves to protect your hands from hot dishes) or potholders

The list above gives you the flexibility to use one set of plates and utensils when the other set is dirty. We have excluded a kettle from this list mainly because it is a more expensive item and the saucepans are a good substitute. Of course, you may wish to buy more items as you become more creative in your cooking activities, and you may need some special items for the preparation of your country's cuisine.

A Food Shopping List For Survival

Bread
Milk
Eggs
Tea or coffee
2 cans of soup
1 box of Total brand cold breakfast cereal
Oil, butter, or margarine
Fruit; bananas and apples are usually cheaper, but oranges and   orange juice are the best sources of Vitamin C
Vegetables of your choice; fresh, frozen, dried, or canned
Salt, pepper, sugar, spices, or other seasonings as desired

Realize that the list above is only for your first day or two, and the prices of these items are usually about the same no matter where you find it convenient to purchase them. The idea is that after taking care of your basic needs, you can then go and visit the larger stores, do some research regarding prices of the food items you want to purchase, and develop a larger shopping list to stock your new kitchen.

A Bathroom Shopping List

Here is a list of items that you can purchase either from the local discount store or from the nearest full-service drugstore (chemist) or a department store.

	One Person	Two People	Two People & Child
Bathmat	1	1	1
Shower curtain & set of rings	1	1	1
Soap ("bars" or "cakes")	1	1	2
Shampoo	1	1	1
Bath towels	2	3	4
Wash cloths or hand towels	2	3	5
Toilet paper, package	1	1	1

Bathmats are placed in front of the bathtub or shower stall to absorb water dripping from a wet person. Shower curtains are hung from railings around a tub or shower, with the lower hem inside the tub to hold water in as you shower. You can use wet wash cloths to scrub your face or body or dry wash cloths or hand towels to dry your face and hands. These items are all washable in a washing machine.

Dress Formality Categories

CASUAL CLOTHING
Shorts for both men and women
Jeans/trousers/unlined pants
Plaid/check/printed shirts
T-shirts/sweatshirts
Low or no-heel shoes/open shoes/sneakers
Light dresses

INFORMAL CLOTHING

Men	Women
Sport coat and pants	Skirt and blouse
White shirt	Dress
Shoes with soft uppers	Dress pants
	Closed shoes, heeled

FORMAL CLOTHING

Men	Women
Two-piece suit: matching coat, pants	Skirt and blouse
White shirt	Dress, mid-length or longer
Tie	Dress pants
Dress shoes	Closed shoes, heeled
National dress	National dress

BLACK TIE

Men	Women
Tuxedo with cummerbund/bowtie	High-fashion skirt and blouse
White shirt	Dress/gown, floor-length
Dress shoes	Closed shoes, heeled
National dress	National dress

This table is a guide; there are many degrees of casual, informal, and formal affected by the style and fabric of the clothing.

International Driver's Licenses

Countries that issue International Driver's Licenses acceptable in the United States are listed below. These were the original signatories to the United Nations Convention on Road Traffic (Geneva, 1949) and the convention on the Regulation of Inter-American Automotive Traffic (Washington, D.C., 1943)

Albania	Egypt	Kampuchea
Algeria	El Salvador	Korea, Rep. of
Andorra	Fiji	Laos
Argentina	Finland	Lebanon
Australia	France	Lesotho
Austria	French Polynesia	Madagascar
Bahamas	Germany, Fed. Rep. of	Malawi
Bangladesh	Ghana	Malaysia
Barbados	Gibraltar	Mali
Belgium	Grenada	Malta
Benin	Guatemala	Martinique
Botswana	Guernsey	Mexico
Brazil	Guinea-Bissau	Monaco
Bulgaria	Guyana	Morocco
Canada	Haiti	Netherlands
Cayman Islands	Honduras	New Caledonia
Central African Rep.	Hong Kong	New Zealand
Chile	Hungary	Nicaragua
Colombia	Iceland	Niger
Congo	India	Norway
Costa Rica	Ireland	Panama
Cuba	Israel	Papua New Guinea
Curacao	Italy	Paraguay
Cyprus	Ivory Coast	Peru
Czechoslovakia	Jamaica	Philippines
Denmark	Japan	Poland
Dominican Republic	Jersey	Portugal
Ecuador	Jordan	Reunion

Romania	Spain	Tunisia
Rwanda	Sri Lanka	Turkey
St. Lucia, St. Vincent	Suriname	U.S.S.R.
St. Pierre & Miquelon	Sweden	United Kingdom
San Marino	Switzerland	Uruguay
Senegal	Syria	Venezuela
Seychelles	Taiwan (Rep. of China)	Vietnam
Sierra Leone	Thailand	West Malaysia
Singapore	Togo	Yugoslavia
South Africa	Trinidad & Tobago	Zaire

Source: *AAA Digest of Motor Laws*, 57th edition, 1991

Voluntary Agencies in Major Cities

A complete directory of voluntary agencies in all cities of the United States is published every three years by the Immigration Outreach Department and can be obtained by writing to them at 425 Eye Street NW, Washington, D.C. 20536. The information in this Appendix is taken from the 1989 directory.

Some organizations listed are termed Qualified Designated Entities (QDEs). They assist applicants seeking to legalize their status. These are marked with a Q in this list and in the directory. Agencies marked with an asterisk are recognized by the Board of Immigration Appeals. An N next to the address shows that this office is the national office.

NEW YORK

International Center of the
Capital Region   (Q)   *
West Mall Office Plaza
875 Central Avenue
Albany, NY 12206
(518) 459-8812

Congress of Racial Equality
1457 Flatbush Avenue
Brooklyn, NY 11210
(718) 343-CORE

Project Ari
Action for Russian
Immigrants
330 Coney Island
Brooklyn, NY 11235
(718) 934-3500

(Q) International Institute of
Buffalo, N.Y. Inc.   (Q)
864 Delaware Avenue
Buffalo, NY 14209
(716) 883-1900

American Council for Nationalities Service (Q) (N)
95 Madison Avenue
New York, NY 10016
(212) 532-5858

Hebrew Immigrant Aid Society (N)
200 Park Avenue South
New York, NY 10016
(212) 967-4100

WASHINGTON, D.C.

Buddhist Vihara Social Charities *
5017 16th Street, NW
Washington, DC 20011
(202) 723-0773

Korean Community Center (Q)
7720 Alaska Avenue, NW
Washington, DC 20012
(202) 882-8270

Lutheran Immigration and Refugee Service
5111 16th Street, NW
Washington, DC 20011
(202) 829-7640

Traveller's Aid Society of Washington D.C. (Q)
1015 12th Street, NW
Washington, DC 20005
(202) 347-0101

Mexican American Legal Defense and Education Fund
1701 18th St., NW
Washington, DC 20009
(202) 628-4074

BOSTON

International Institute (Q)
287 Commonwealth Avenue
Boston, MA 02115
(617) 536-1081

Volunteer Lawyers Project
73 Tremont Street
Boston, MA 02108
(617) 742-5823

CHICAGO

Assyrian Universal Alliance (Q)
7055 North Clark
Chicago, IL 60626
(312) 274-9262

American Filipino Professionals Civic Alliance (Q)
2245 North Southport Avenue
Chicago, IL 60614
(312) 549-0909

Japanese American Service Committee of Chicago
4427 North Clark Street
Chicago, IL 60640
(312) 275-7212

Travellers and Immigrants Aid of Chicago (Q) *
1950 North Milwaukee
Chicago, IL 60640
(312) 489-7303

YMCA of the USA (N)
International Division
Refugee Services Office
101 North Wacker Drive
Chicago, IL 60606
(312) 977-0031

SAN FRANCISCO

Catholic Social Services *
2940 16th Street, Room 206
San Francisco, CA 94103
(415) 861-2387

International Institute (Q) *
2209 Van Ness Avenue
San Francisco, CA 94103
(415) 673-1720

La Raza Centro Legal *
2588 Mission Street
San Francisco, CA 94110
(415) 526-5506

Church World Service
Immigration and Refugee
Program *
942 Market Street, Suite 712
San Francisco, CA 94109
(415) 982-6630

United States Catholic
Conference (Q) *
Migration and Refugee Services
582 Market Street
San Francisco, CA 94104
(415) 362-8677

LOS ANGELES

Center for Employment
Training, Inc. (Q)
2947 East 44th Street
Los Angeles, CA 90058
(213) 582-9789

Catholic Charities (Q)
Immigration and Citizenship
1400 West Ninth Street
Los Angeles, CA 90015-0095
(213) 251-3442 or 251-3489

International Institute (Q)
435 South Boyle Avenue
Los Angeles, CA 90033
(213) 264-6210

World Relief (Q)
Highland Park Church of God
6209 Rubie Street
Los Angeles, CA 90012
(213) 257-7561 or 257-7595

MIAMI

Private Immigration
Agency (PIA) (Q) (N)
7880-B Biscayne Boulevard
Miami, FL 33138
(305) 751-8212 or 751-8217
or 854-4950

DETROIT

International Institute (Q) *
4138 West Vernon Avenue
Detroit, MI 48202
(313) 871-8600

SER-JOBS for Progress (Q)
9301 Michigan Avenue
Detroit, MI 48209
(313) 846-2240

Important Dates in the United States

Events listed without a specific date in parentheses are dates that vary from year to year. Dates marked with an asterisk (*) are national holidays observed by all organizations. Banks and government offices are likely to observe additional holidays. (G) means a gift-giving holiday, with the third column listing to whom gifts are usually given. Gifts to teachers and people higher in rank should not be given without consulting with your colleagues.

Month	Holiday Name (Date)	Gifts to
January	New Year's Day (1) * Martin Luther King, Jr.'s Birthday (15)	
February	Lincoln's Birthday (12) Valentine's Day (14) (G) President's Day	Sweethearts
March	St. Patrick's Day (17)	
April	Easter Passover Secretaries' Day (G)	Secretaries
May	Mother's Day (G) Armed Forces Day Memorial Day * Flag Day (14)	Mothers
June	Father's Day (G)	Fathers
July	Independence Day (4) *	
August		
September	Labor Day (First Monday) * Grandparents' Day (G) Rosh Hashona	Grandparents
October	Columbus Day Halloween (31)	

November	Election Day	
	Veteran's Day (11)	
	Thanksgiving Day *	
December	Hanukkah (G)	Children/ General
	Christmas (25) * (G)	Children/ General
	New Year's Eve (31)	

American Cooking Terms

Bake: to put an ovenproof dish of food inside an oven with the heat turned on. Ignore the "preheat" setting on an electric stove if you wish to save electricity. Most baking is done at an oven temperature between 325 degrees and 400 degrees Fahrenheit. Reheating previously baked items is usually done at 350 degrees.

Baste: the action of moistening anything that is cooking (usually meat) with drippings or butter.

Boil: to cook in hot liquid. Unless a different liquid is specified, fill a saucepan with water, turn one of the surface burners of the stove to "high," and place the saucepan on it.

Broil: to put a dish inside an oven with only the upper coils heated in an electric stove or with only the broiler section gas flame turned on in a gas stove. This is usual for cooking steak, chicken, or fish or for browning a dish after microwave cooking is complete.

Deep-fry: to cook in ½ to 2 cups of oil.

Fry: to cook in a little oil (not more than 2 tablespoons).

Poach: to cook in water that is kept hot but not allowed to boil. It usually applies to cooking eggs without fat or to cooking fruit for sauces.

Roast: a term used for cooking meat. It means placing a large piece of meat fat side up in a shallow pan in the middle of the oven and baking it slowly, uncovered.

Appendix 193

Glossary

International English	American English
aerial (radio/TV)	antenna
alsatian	German shepherd/police dog
anorak	parka
articulated lorry	trailer truck
aubergine	eggplant
autumn	fall
bank holiday	legal holiday
banknote	bill
bap	hamburger bun
bat (ping pong)	paddle
bath (noun)	bathtub
bath (verb)	bathe
bed-sit	studio
bespoke/made to measure	custom made
big dipper	roller coaster
bill	check (in a restaurant)
bill/account	account
billion = million million	billion = thousand million
biscuit (sweet)	cookie
biscuit (unsweetened)	cracker
black or white? (milk/cream in coffee)	with or without?
blackleg	scab
black treacle	molasses
blind (window)	shade, venetian blind
block of flats	apartment house/building
blue jeans	dungarees
bomb (success)	bomb (disaster)
bonnet (car)	hood (car), woman's hat
book (verb)	make a reservation
boot (car)	trunk/rear deck
bootlace/shoelace	shoestring
bottom drawer	hope chest
bowler/hard hat	derby
box room	lumber room
braces	suspenders
break (school)	recess
bridge roll	hot dog bun
briefs	shorts or jockey shorts
broad bean	lima bean

International English	American English
butter muslin/cheese cloth	cheese cloth
candy floss	cotton candy
caravan	trailer
caretaker/porter	janitor
car park	parking lot
catapult	slingshot
cattlegrid	Texas gate
centre (city/business)	downtown/main street
centre reservation	median strip/divider
chairman (business)	president, chief executive
chemist	druggist
chemist's shop	pharmacy/drugstore
chest of drawers	bureau/dresser
chicory	endive
chips	French fries
chocolate/sweets	candy
cinema	movie house/theater
class/form (school)	grade
cloakroom	check room
cloakroom attendant	hat check person
clothes peg	clothes pin
collar stiffener	collar stay
collar stud	collar button
conscription (army)	draft
contraceptive	rubber, condom
convoy	procession, caravan
cooker	stove
corn flour	corn starch
corporation	city/municipal government
cot/crib	baby bed/crib
cotton	thread
cotton reel	spool
cotton wool	cotton batting/cotton wads/ absorbent cotton
courgettes	zucchini
court shoe	pump
cow gum	rubber cement
cream cracker	soda cracker
credentials	qualifications
crisps	chips (potato)
cul-de-sac	dead end
cupboard	closet
curtains	drapes
dessicated (coconut)	shredded

International English	American English
diamante	rhinestone
directory enquiries	information/directory assistance
district	precinct
diversion	detour
drain (indoors)	sewer pipe/soil pipe
draper	dry goods store
draught excluder	weather stripping
draughts	checkers
drawing pin	thumbtack
dress circle	mezzanine/loge
dressing gown	bathrobe
dual carriageway	divided highway
dummy	pacifier
dungarees	overalls
dustbin/bin	garbage can/trash can/ash can
dynamo	generator
earth wire/earth	ground wire
eiderdown	comforter
endive	chicory
Esq./Mr.	Mr.
estate agent	realtor
estate car	station wagon
face flannel	washcloth
fair (fun)	carnival
filling station	gas station
film	movie
first floor	second floor
fish slice	pancake spatula/turner
fitted carpet	wall-to-wall carpet
flat	apartment
flex	electric cord/wire
fly-over	overpass
football/soccer	soccer
fortnight	two weeks
foyer	lobby/foyer
full stop (punc.)	period
funny bone	crazy bone
gallery	balcony
gangway	aisle
gaol	jail
garden	yard
gear lever	gear shift

International English	American English
geyser (gas)	water heater
goods truck (railway)	freight truck
goose pimples	goose bumps
gramophone/record player	phonograph/record player
green fingers	green thumb
green pepper/capsicum	bell pepper/green pepper/ sweet pepper
grill	broil
guard (railway)	conductor
gym shoes/plimsolls/tennis shoes	sneakers/tennis shoes
haberdashery	notions
hair grip/kirby grip	bobbie pin
hair slide	barette
handbag	purse/pocket book
hardware	housewares
headmaster/headmistress	principal
hire purchase	time payment/installment plan
holiday	vacation
homely-pleasant	homely-ugly
hoover (noun)	vacuum cleaner
hoover (verb)	vacuum
housing estate	sub-division
ice/sorbet	sherbet
iced lolly	popsicle
icing sugar	powdered sugar/confectioner's sugar
identification parade	lineup
immersion heater (electric)	water heater
interval (film)	intermission
ironmonger	hardware store
item/unit (of production)	widget
jab (injection)	shot
joint (meat)	roast
jug	pitcher
jumble sale	rummage sale
jumper/sweater/pullover	sweater/pullover
kiosk (telephone/cigarette)	booth (telephone)
kipper	smoked herring
knock up (tennis)	warm up
label	tag
larder	pantry
lavatory/toilet/W.C.	toilet/john/bathroom

International English	American English
lay-by	pull-off
leader	
leading article in newspaper	editorial
1st violin in orchestra	concert master
left luggage office	baggage room
let	lease/rent
level crossing (railway)	grade crossing
lift	elevator
limited	incorporated
liver sausage	liverwurst
living room	den
lodger	roomer
lorry	truck
lost property	lost and found
lounge suit	business suit
mackintosh	raincoat
marrow	squash (similar)
methylated spirits	denatured alcohol
mileometer	odometer
mince	hamburger meat
mincer	meat grinder
moped	motorbike
motorway	freeway/throughway/super highway
nappy	diaper
neat (drink)	neat/straight/straight up
net curtains	sheers/under drapes
newsagent	newsdealer/newsstand
nought	zero or "Oh"
noughts and crosses	tic-tac-toe
number plate	license plate
off license/wine merchant	liquor store
off-side lane	right-hand lane nearest center of road, in U.K.
oven cloth/gloves	potholders/gloves
overtake (vehicle)	pass
pack (of cards)	deck
packed lunch	bag lunch, sack lunch
pantechnicon	moving van
pants	shorts (underwear)
paraffin (oil)	kerosene
parcel	package/packet
pavement/footpath	sidewalk

International English	American English
pelmet	valence
personal call	person-to-person
petrol	gas
pillar box	mail box/mail drop
plain cake	pound cake
plus-fours	knickers
point/power point	outlet/socket
post (verb)	mail (verb)
postal code	zip code
postbox	mailbox
postman	mailman/letter carrier
postponement	raincheck
pram	baby carriage/baby buggy
press studs	snaps
prison	penitentiary
prostitute/tart/whore	tramp/call girl/hooker/street walker
pub	tavern/saloon
public convenience	rest room/toilet/comfort station
public school/private school	private school
pudding	dessert
purse	change purse
pushchair	stroller
put down/entered (goods bought)	charged
put through (telephone)	connected
quay	wharf/pier
queue (noun)	line
queue (verb)	stand in line/line up
rasher (bacon)	slice
reception (hotel)	front desk
receptionist	desk clerk
return ticket	round trip
reverse charges	call collect
reversing lights	back-up lights
ring up	call/phone
robin (small red-breasted bird, symbol of Christmas)	robin (large red-breasted bird, symbol of spring)
roof/hood (car)	top
roundabout (road)	traffic circle
rubber	eraser
rubbish	garbage/trash
saloon (car)	sedan

International English	American English
scribbling pad/block	scratch pad
sellotape	scotch tape
semi-detached	duplex
semolina	cream of wheat
service flats	apartment hotel
settee	love seat
shop	store
shop assistant	sales clerk/salesperson
shopwalker	floorwalker
sideboard	buffet
sideboards (hair)	sideburns
silencer (car)	muffler
single ticket	one-way ticket
sitting room/lounge/drawing room	living room
skipping rope	jump rope
skirting board	baseboard
sledge/toboggan	sled
sleeping car	pullman/sleeper
smalls (washing)	underwear
sofa	davenport/couch
solicitor	lawyer/attorney
sorbet	sherbet
spanner	monkey wrench
spirits (drink)	liquor
spring onion	scallion (similar)
staff (academic)	faculty
stake (wooden)	post
stalls (theatre)	orchestra seats
stand (for public office)	run
standard lamp	floor lamp
state school	public school
sticking plaster	adhesive tape
stone (fruit)	pit
sultana	raisin
sump (car)	oil pan
surgery (doctor's/dentist's)	office
surgical spirit	rubbing alcohol
suspender belt	garter belt
suspenders	garters
swede	turnip/rutabaga
sweet shop/confectioner	candy store
sweets/chocolate	candy
Swiss roll	jelly roll

International English	American English
tadpole	pollywog
tap	faucet
teat (baby's)	nipple
tea trolley	tea cart
telegram	wire
term (academic)	semester
things	stuff
tights	pantyhose
timetable	schedule
tin	can
tip (n. and v.)	dump
torch	flashlight
traffic lights	stop lights/traffic signals/stop signals
trousers	pants/slacks
truncheon (police)	night stick
trunk call	long distance
tube/underground	subway
turn-ups (trousers)	cuffs (pants)
undergraduates:	
1st year	freshman
2nd year	sophomore
3rd year	junior
4th year	senior
unit trust	mutual fund
upper circle	first balcony
valve (radio)	tube
van	delivery truck
van (car type)	panel truck
vest	undershirt
visually position	eyeball (verb)
waistcoat	vest
wallet	billfold
wardrobe	closet
wash up	do the dishes
wash your hands	wash up
Welsh dresser	hutch
windcheater	windbreaker
windscreen	windshield
wing/mudguard	fender
Woolworths	dime store/five and ten
zed	zee

From *American English/English American*, Anthea Bickerton (Abson Books, 1990, with some additions)

Clothing Sizes—U.S. and Metric

Women's Coats and Dresses
Continental	34	36	38	40	42	44	46	48
U.S.	6	8	10	12	14	16	18	20

Women's Blouses and Sweaters
Continental	40	42	44	46	48	50
U.S.	32	34	36	38	40	42

Women's Shoes
Continental	35	35½	36	36½	37	38	39	40
U.S.	4	4½	5	5½	6	7, 7½	8	9

Women's Stockings
Continental	0	1	2	3	4	5
U.S.	8	8½	9	9½	10	10½

Men's Suits and Coats
Continental	44	46	48	50	52	54	56
U.S.	34	36	38	40	42	44	46

Men's Shirts
Continental	36	37	38	39	41	42	43
U.S.	14	14½	15	15½	16	16½	17

Men's Shoes
Continental	39	40	41	42	43	44
U.S.	7	7½	8	8½, 9	9½, 10	10½

Continental	45	46
U.S.	11, 11½	12, 12½

Men's Socks
Continental	39	40	41	42	43	44	45
U.S.	9½	10	10½	11	11½	12	12½

Men's Hats
Continental	53	54	55	56	57	58	59
U.S.	6⅝	6¾	6⅞	7	7⅛	7¼	7⅜

Children's Clothing
  Measurements vary considerably from store to store. Some sizes refer to age, others are arbitrary.

From: *The New York Public Library Desk Reference 1989* (Prentice Hall, 1989)

U.S. Customary Weights and Measures/ Metric Conversions

Liquids
1 liter   = 1.057 quarts
1 milliliter = 0.034 fluid ounces
5 milliliters = 0.17 fluid ounces ≅ 1 teaspoon
15 milliliters = 0.51 fluid ounces ≅ 1 tablespoon
30 milliliters = 1.02 fluid ounces ≅ ⅛ cup
50 milliliters = 1.70 fluid ounces
60 milliliters = 2.04 fluid ounces ≅ ¼ cup
78 milliliters = 2.66 fluid ounces ≅ ⅓ cup
100 milliliters = 3.4 fluid ounces
120 milliliters = 4.08 fluid ounces ≅ ½ cup
156 milliliters = 5.3 fluid ounces ≅ ⅔ cup
177 milliliters = 6.02 fluid ounces ≅ ¾ cup
200 milliliters = 6.8 fluid ounces
235 milliliters = 7.99 fluid ounces ≅ 1 cup
250 milliliters = 8.45 fluid ounces

Dry Measures
1   gram   =   .035 ounce
28   grams   =   .98 ounce ≅ 1 ounce
50   grams   = 1.75 ounces
100   grams   = 3.52 ounces
114   grams   = 3.99 ounces ≅ ¼ pound
200   grams   = 7 ounces
228   grams   = 7.98 ounces ≅ ½ pound
343   grams   = 12.0 ounces ≅ ¾ pound
454   grams   = 15.9 ounces ≅ 1 pound
500   grams   = 17.6 ounces ≅ 1.1 pounds
                  = 1 pound + 1.6 ounces
1   kilogram   = 2.2 pounds
5   kilograms = 11 pounds
10   kilograms = 22 pounds
22.73 kilograms = 50 pounds
45.45 kilograms = 100 pounds
50   kilograms = 110 pounds
100   kilograms = 220 pounds

Length Measures

1	millimeter	= .039 inches
1	centimeter	= .3937 inches
1.27	centimeter	= .50 inches = ½ inch
2.00	centimer	= .7874 inches
2.54	centimeter	= 1.0 inches
30.48	centimeter	= 12 inches = 1 foot
91.44	centimeter	= 36 inches = 3 feet = 1 yard
1	meter	= 39 inches
1.524	meters	= 5 feet
1.828	meters	= 6 feet (tall person)
3.048	meters	= 10 feet (one-story building)
5	meters	= 19.5 feet
10	meters	= 32.5 feet

Suggested Reading

American Ways: A Guide for Foreigners in the United States. Gary Althen. Intercultural Press, 1988.

The Art of Crossing Cultures. Craig Storti. Intercultural Press, 1990.

Belonging in America. Constance Perrin. University of Wisconsin Press, 1990.

Cultural Misunderstandings: The French-American Experience. Raymonde Carroll. Translated by Carol Volk. University of Chicago Press, 1988.

The Culture Puzzle: Cross-cultural Communication for English as a Second Language. Deena Levine, Jim Baxter, and Piper McNulty. Prentice Hall, 1987.

Culture Shock USA. Esther Wanning. Graphic Arts Publishing, 1990.

Curious Customs: The Stories Behind 296 Popular American Rituals. Tad Tuleja. Harmony Books, 1987.

Democracy in America. Alexis de Tocqueville. English translation by George Lawrence, Harper & Row. 1966.

Doublespeak. William Lutz. Harper Collins, 1990.

Letitia Baldridge's Complete Guide to the New Manners for the 90s. Macmillan, 1990.

Living in the U.S.A. 4th ed. Alison R. Lanier. Intercultural Press, 1988.

New Americans—An Oral History—Immigrants and Refugees in the U.S. Today. Al Santoli. Ballantine Books, 1988.

Prescription Drugs. Editors of Consumer's Guide. Signet Books, 1991.

The Ropes to Skip and the Ropes to Know: The Inner Life of an Organization. R. Richard Ritti and G. Ray Funkhouser. John Wiley, 1987.

Slang: The Topic by Topic Dictionary of Contemporary American Lingos. Paul Dickson. Pocket Books, 1990.

Student Survival Guide: How to Work Smarter Not Harder. The College Board. 1991.

The Starving Students' Cookbook. Dede Napoli. Warner Books, 1982.

Your Medical Rights. Charles Binlander and Eugene Pavalon. Little, Brown and Co., 1990.

Suggested Videotapes

Here is a list of movies that most Americans are familiar with and that will help you understand some American cultural metaphors. Americans may use lines from these classics or refer to their heroes and heroines as role models.

1776. Director: Peter Hunt. 1972.

Casablanca. Director: Michael Curtiz. 1942. Black and white.

Citizen Kane. Director: Orson Welles. 1941. Black and white.

Gone with the Wind. Director: Victor Fleming. 1939.

It's a Wonderful Life. Director: Frank Capra. 1946. Black and white. (Also available colorized.)

The Long Voyage Home. Director: John Ford. 1940. Black and white.

South Pacific. Director: Joshua Logan. 1958.

Summer of '42. Director: Robert Mulligan. 1971.

Yankee Doodle Dandy. Director: Michael Curtiz. 1942. Black and white.

Wizard of Oz. Director: Victor Fleming. 1939.

The following movies will introduce you to American perceptions of contemporary American history and the role of the press.

Broadcast News. Director: James L. Brooks. 1987.

Glory. Director: Edward Zwick. 1989

Guess Who's Coming to Dinner. Director: Stanley Kramer. 1967.

Long Walk Home. Director: Richard Pearce. 1990.

Network. Director: Sidney Lumet. 1976.

Platoon. Director: Oliver Stone. 1986.

And finally, here are a few films that describe the foreign student or immigrant experience in America.

Avalon. Director: Barry Levinson. 1990. (Jewish immigrant experience)

Cold Water. Director: Noriko Ogami. 1987. Available from Intercultural Press. (Documentary describing the foreign student experience)

Come See the Paradise. Director: Alan Parker. 1990. (Japanese-American experience during World War II)

Milagro Beanfield War. Director: Robert Redford. 1988. (Hispanic-American experience in the American Southwest)

Mississippi Masala. Director: Mira Nair. 1991. (East-Indian immigrant experience)

Moonstruck. Director: Norman Jewison. 1987 (Comedy set in the Italian American community)

Green Card. Director: Peter Weir. 1990 (French immigrant experience; comedy. For maximum information, view this tape in conjunction with your reading of *Cultural Misunderstandings*.)

Except as noted, all the videotapes in this listing are available at video rental stores.

Index

Abortion: debate, 164; pill (RU486), 45; right to, 132
Accidents, 134, 172; bicycle, 37; car, 39, 116, 119-120, 172; home, 170; prevention, 170-171
Address, polite forms of, 10; Addresses, finding street, 28, 29, 36
Addressing a letter, 30; domestic, 31; international, 33
AIDS (acquired immune deficiency syndrome), 133
Alcohol: availability, 17; legal age, 14; home use, 19, 53
Alcoholism, 177; drunken driving, 40; grounds for divorce, 157; treatment, Alcoholics Anonymous, 177
American Automobile Assoc. (AAA), 39, 114-115, 116, 117, 166
American accent, described, 6
AMTRAK trains, 42
Animal sacrifice, 165
Answering machines, 26, 29, 168
Appliances, 2, 168; breakdown, repair, cleaning, 69, 79, 107, 167, 170; large kitchen, 68, 69, 79; small, 68; voltage, 2; with rental premises, 54, 57
Apprenticeships, 107, 110
Assault, 112-113, 172-173, 176; prevention, 11
Assistantships, graduate, 98
ATMs (automated teller machines), 142-143

Attorney. *See* Lawyer
Banks and banking, 135-145; loans, 115; reporting to government, 138, 146
Bars and nightclubs, 17-18
Bereavement fare, airline, 159
Better Business Bureau, 102, 147
Biculturalism, 181-182
Births, U.S. laws and customs, 157-158
Book clubs, commercial, 146
Borrowing: items, 78-79; money (loan), 114-115, 136, 145
Buses, Greyhound, 40-41
Business: buying, 108; card, 10; conversation, 26-27; dressing for, 92-94; letters, 31-32; women in, 90, 111-112
Car: accident, 119; borrowing, 53; buying, 114-115; care, 116-117; driving, 38-39; insurance, 116; locked, 166; parking, 51; renting, 39; safety, 118; theft, 119, 172
Chador, 84
Checks and checking, 138-142; cashing businesses, 136
Chemist (drugstore, pharmacy), 63, 122
Child abuse: reporting, 175; prevention, 176
Children: age for marriage, 155; citizenship, 158; cultural adjustment, 83; discussions about, 24; housing for families with, 56, 58;

marriage of, 154-155; as proof of marriage, 156; medical care of; 123, 129; parties for, 19; public behavior, 21
Churches, U.S., 159-163
Cigarette smoking, 9, 170
Citizenship, in relation to: banking, 138; children, 158; divorce, 157; the law, 120; military draft 30; marriage, 155-156; Social Security, 13; taxes, 145; work, 97-101, 104, 106
Clothing, 83-95
Communist party, 5
Con-artists, 101
Constitution, U.S., 5, 159
Consumer Reports, 115
Conversational etiquette, 23-25, 43, 45
Coupons, discount, 64
Credit, 52; cards, 39, 47, 144; unions, 136, 138
Crime Victim Compensation Program, 172
Cults, religious, 162
Curriculum vitae (bio-data, résumé), 99
Customs Service, U.S., 2, 4-6
Death: funerals, dressing for, 95; legal considerations, 158-159; sacrificial, 165; wills, 148
Delicatessen (deli) food, 63
Dental care, 129-130
Deportation, 5, 45
Depression, mental, 152, 178
Directions, travel, 35-37
Divorce, 156-157, 176-177
Doctors (physicians), 2, 120, 123-131, 144, 164, 175, 178
Driver's license, international, 1; obtaining U.S., 38-39
Drugs: addiction, 177; illegal, 2, 45; medications, 122

Earrings, American attitude toward, 91
800 toll-free telephone nos., 13, 42, 175, 177, 178
Electricity, 2, 167-168
Emergencies, 166-173; auto service, 117-118; emergency ward, hospital, 126; life-threatening, 127; medical center (clinic), 82, 121, 122; telephone number (911), 127, 169-173; telegrams, 34
Employment, 96-113
Encyclopedia of Associations, 108
English as a Second Language (ESL), 6
Equal Opportunity, Office of, 105, 112
Equality: legal, 111; of opportunity, 23, 154; of roommates, 52; of sexes, 153-154, 156
Ethics: stealing, 14, 76; telephone card use, 30; vs. morality, 160; welfare, 150
Eyeglasses or contact lenses, 2
Family, 53; business, 108; breakup of, 157; meal, in American home, 18, 19, 51, 72, 94; name, 10, 158; separation from, 12, 175-176; restaurants, 18; members, care of, 129, 132, 134, 147, 150, 159, 177; topic of conversation, 24; how long to stay with, 46; temporary housing for, 58; poverty level income, 149; transferring money to, 137; women's role in, 153, 177
Family problems, help for, 175-178
Faucet (tap), hot and cold water, 9; leaking, what to do, 166;

Federal Express, commercial shipping service, 34
Fingerprinting, 13, 164
Fire: emergency, 170; prevention, 169-170;
First Amendment, U.S. Constitution, 13, 159
Food, 14-22, 60-72; on airlines, 2, 44; on buses, 41; coffee, 22; dietary restrictions, 2, 19, 44, 65; fast food, 14; take-out, 14, 57; tea, 22; sharing, 52
Foreign Medical Graduates Association, 108
Frequent flyer tickets, 44
Form 1040, income tax, 145
Freedom, 12, 13, 84, 85, 91, 111, 145, 159, 163
Freedom from Religion Foundation, 160
Friends: borrowing from, 79, 145; help from, 56, 100, 102, 106, 123, 138, 150, 169, 178; making, 9, 10, 12, 17, 18, 23-25, 48, 110; meeting, on arrival, 3-4, 35; parties, 19, 51; shelter, 46, 152; touching, 154
Furniture, 50, 51, 53, 56, 57, 58; rental, 57-58
Gambling, 147
Glasses or contact lenses, 2
Goodwill stores, 58
Grace (blessing before meals), 19
Green Card, 98
Greyhound Package Express (GPX), 41
Hairstyles and headcoverings, 83-85
Hierarchy: in business, 110; in fabrics, 90; in modes of travel, 37; psychological, 111
Hippies, 149

HMO (Health Maintenance Organization), 128
Holidays: legal, 97; religious, 164; vacation, 97
Homeopathy, 124
Homosexuality, 112, 154
Hot dogs, 65-66
Housing, 46-59
Humor, interpretation, 24, 43
Illegal: behavior in hotels, 47; business practices, 102, 138, 147, 158; discrimination in housing, 48, 58; drugs, 45; entry, 174; games of chance, 147; hiring practices, 97, 104; polygamy, 162; religious practices, 165
Immigration: advisers, 151; clearing, 3, 4-6, 45; INS, 13; and marriage, 155-157; questioning, 174-175; and working, 96-99
Income tax returns, 145
Insect problems, 81-82
Insurance: adjusters, 120; car, 116; dental 130; life, 147-148; medical, 127-129, 159; property loss, 172
Internal Revenue Service, U.S., 146
International: driver's license, 1, 38, 39; letters, 33; money orders, 136-137; telephone calls, 25, 47, 52
Jewelry, 2, 91; as collateral, 145; safety of, 12, 33, 168, 170
Jobs. *See* Employment
Kafiyeh, 84
Kitchens, 50, 52, 54, 60, 63, 67, 68, 77, 79, 81, 152; safety in, 166-170
Landlords, 46-59
Language, American, 6
Laundromat, 75
Lawyer (attorney): educa-

tional equivalency, 108; immigration, 151; personal injury, 120; prenuptial agreement, 156; right to consult, 174; wills, preparation, 134, 148
Leasing: apartment, 52, 55, 56-57; car, 115
Left luggage, 44
Legal Aid Society, 148, 176
Loans: car, 114-115; consumer, 136; housing, 136; as proof of marriage, 156; personal, 145
Lotteries. *See* Gambling
Mailbox rental, 30
Maps, 35-37
Marriage, 18, 24, 154-156, 165
Medical care, 120, 121-134
Medications, 2, 122, 123
Men and women, relations between, 18, 19, 111-113, 153-157, 165, 173
Microwave oven, 68-69
Military draft registration, 30
Miscegenation, 156
Missionaries, 163
Money, 11; currency, U.S., 7-8; exchange, 6, 44, 47; management, 135-152; orders, 136
Monoculturalism, 180-181
Morality. *See* Ethics
Mugging (street assault), 172
Name: brand, 2, 123; child, 157-158; country, 33; personal, 1, 10, 26, 64, 113, 116, 140, 168, 181
National dress, wearing of, 83, 84, 91, 94
911 emergency phone no., 127, 169-173
Ounce, types of, 70
Ovens, cooking, 68-69, 170
Overnight mail, 34
Overseas mail, 33-34

Parents Anonymous, 175-176
Parties, 19, 94
Pay telephone, 27
Permanent resident: laws regarding, 98-99; marriage and, 155
Pets, 51, 56
Physicians. *See* Doctors
Plumbing, 166
Plunger, sink, toilet, 166
Police, crime dispatch policy, 171-172
Post Office, U.S., 30-34
Privacy, 10, 23-24, 49, 50, 53, 125, 134
Professional equivalency requirements, 107-108
Quacks, 125
Racism, 11, 48, 111, 156
Rape, 112-113, 173, 176
Real estate, 46; agents, 55-56
Religion, 159-165
Restaurants, 14
Responsibility and obligations, 29, 38, 45, 67, 76, 52, 79, 132-133, 135, 142-144, 146, 147, 151, 153, 175
Résumé (curriculum vitae), 99
Rights 4, 23, 120, 140, 163; abortion, 164; animal, 90, 165; child, 175; civil, 111, 174; handicapped, 149; to life, 164; patient, 124, 131-132; privacy, 163, 175; telephone subscriber, 29; tenant, 52, 59; women's, 111-112, 154, 176
Room rental, 49-53
RU486 pills, 45
Sabbath observance, 163-164
Safety, in home, 168-171
Sales: cars, 115; rummage, 58; in stores, 95
Sales jobs, 101
Salvation Army store, 58
Seasons of the year, 86

Secular society, 159-160
Sexual diseases, 133
Shopping, 60-67, 68-69, 86-91
Smells and odors: American, 10; clean, 73; cooking, 51; dangerous, 170
Smoking, 9, 170
Social Security, 13, 175
Sponsor, 5, 48, 49, 99, 128, 145, 151
Stamps, postage, 31-32
Stereotypes, 11, 112, 153
Street addresses, 28, 29, 36
Studio apartment, 53
Supreme Court, 163-165
Swimming pools, 122
Taboos: homosexuality, 112, 154; religious practices, 165; topics, 23, 24, 45
Tadung, 84
Tampons, 73-74
Taxes, 97; charity deduction, 152; filing requirements, 145-146; preparers, 107
Taxis, 6-8
Telemarketing, 152
Telephone manners, 25-27, 49, 52, 53, 102
Television, 13, 57, 73, 76, 129
Time, U.S. attitudes toward, 9, 18, 23, 26, 27, 64, 65, 69, 100, 105, 107, 110, 113, 139, 145, 150, 151
Tipping, 14, 15, 18, 40
Toilet (bathroom, rest room), 9, 50, 54, 74, 122; in buses, 42; cleaning, 53, 80
Trains, 42
Translator (interpreter), 127
Travel agent, 43
Traveler's Aid, 4, 35, 44
Traveler's checks, 3, 44
Turban, 84
TWA vs. Hardison, 164
United Parcel Service (UPS), 34

University: assistantships, 98; ESL, 6; exercise centers, 122; food, 14, 16; health insurance requirements, 128-129; housing, 46, 49, 50, 58; jobs, 97; medical clinics, 122; safety, 127
Used Car Buying Guide, 115
Vacuum cleaning, 78-79
Victim Compensation Program, Crime, 172
Visa, 1, 44-45, 158; fiance(é), 155; H-1 training, 98; student, 97
Volunteering, 100, 150, 152
W.C. *See* Toilet
Washing: clothes 74-77; dishes, 69
Water flow problems, 166
Welfare, 46, 150, 175
White Pages, 28
Wills: estate, 134, 148; living, 133-134
Window treatments, 58
Women, 2, 9, 10, 11, 73, 85, 89, 90, 122, 176; conversing, 19; finances, 135, 148; and food, 18, 20, 71; medical, 73, 123, 125, 134; touching, 154
Women and men, relations between, 153-157
Work. *See* Employment
Xenophobia (fear of foreigners), 111
Yarmulke, 84
Yellow Pages, 28
YMCA and YWCA, 48
Youth hostels, 48

Other Books from John Muir Publications

Adventure Vacations: From Trekking in New Guinea to Swimming in Siberia, Bangs 256 pp. $17.95
Asia Through the Back Door, 3rd ed., Steves and Gottberg 326 pp. $15.95
Belize: A Natural Destination, Mahler, Wotkyns, Schafer 304 pp. $16.95
Bus Touring: Charter Vacations, U.S.A., Warren with Bloch 168 pp. $9.95
California Public Gardens: A Visitor's Guide, Sigg 304 pp. $16.95
Catholic America: Self-Renewal Centers and Retreats, Christian-Meyer 325 pp. $13.95
Costa Rica: A Natural Destination, 2nd ed., Sheck 288 pp. $16.95
Elderhostels: The Students' Choice, 2nd ed., Hyman 312 pp. $15.95
Environmental Vacations: Volunteer Projects to Save the Planet, 2nd ed., Ocko 248 pp. $16.95
Europe 101: History & Art for the Traveler, 4th ed., Steves and Openshaw 372 pp. $15.95
Europe Through the Back Door, 10th ed., Steves 448 pp. $16.95
A Foreign Visitor's Guide to America, Baldwin and Levine 200 pp. $10.95 (avail. 9/92)
Floating Vacations: River, Lake, and Ocean Adventures, White 256 pp. $17.95
Great Cities of Eastern Europe, Rapoport 256 pp. $16.95
Gypsying After 40: A Guide to Adventure and Self-Discovery, Harris 264 pp. $14.95
The Heart of Jerusalem, Nellhaus 336 pp. $12.95
Indian America: A Traveler's Companion, 2nd ed., Eagle/Walking Turtle 448 pp. $17.95
Interior Furnishings Southwest: The Sourcebook of the Best Production Craftspeople, Deats and Villani 256 pp. $19.95 (avail. 9/92)
Mona Winks: Self-Guided Tours of Europe's Top Museums, Steves and Openshaw 456 pp. $14.95
Opera! The Guide to Western Europe's Great Houses, Zietz 296 pp. $18.95
Paintbrushes and Pistols: How the Taos Artists Sold the West, Taggett and Schwarz 280 pp. $17.95
The People's Guide to Mexico, 8th ed., Franz 608 pp. $17.95
The People's Guide to RV Camping in Mexico, Franz with Rogers 320 pp. $13.95
Ranch Vacations: The Complete Guide to Guest and Resort, Fly-Fishing, and Cross-Country Skiing Ranches, 2nd ed., Kilgore 396 pp. $18.95
The Shopper's Guide to Art and Crafts in the Hawaiian Islands, Schuchter 272 pp. $13.95
The Shopper's Guide to Mexico, Rogers and Rosa 224 pp. $9.95
Ski Tech's Guide to Equipment, Skiwear, and Accessories, ed. Tanler 144 pp. $11.95
Ski Tech's Guide to Maintenance and Repair, ed. Tanler 160 pp. $11.95
A Traveler's Guide to Asian Culture, Chambers 224 pp. $13.95
Traveler's Guide to Healing Centers and Retreats in North America, Rudee and Blease 240 pp. $11.95
Understanding Europeans, Miller 272 pp. $14.95
Undiscovered Islands of the Caribbean, 2nd ed., Willes 232 pp. $14.95
Undiscovered Islands of the Mediterranean, 2nd ed., Moyer and Willes 256 pp. $13.95
Undiscovered Islands of the U.S. and Canadian West Coast, Moyer and Willes 208 pp. $12.95
A Viewer's Guide to Art: A Glossary of Gods, People, and Creatures, Shaw and Warren 144 pp. $10.95

2 to 22 Days Series
Each title offers 22 flexible daily itineraries that can be used to get the most out of vacations of any length. Included are not only "must see" attractions but also little-known villages and hidden "jewels" as well as valuable general information.
22 Days Around the World, 1992 ed., Rapoport and Willes 256 pp. $12.95 (1993 ed. avail. 8/92)
2 to 22 Days Around the Great Lakes, 1992 ed., Schuchter 192 pp. $9.95

22 Days in Alaska, Lanier 128 pp. $7.95
2 to 22 Days in the American Southwest, 1992 ed., Harris 176 pp. $9.95
2 to 22 Days in Asia, 1992 ed., Rapoport and Willes 176 pp. $9.95 (**1993 ed.** avail. 8/92)
2 to 22 Days in Australia, 1992 ed., Gottberg 192 pp. $9.95 (**1993 ed.** avail. 8/92)
2 to 22 Days in California, 1992 ed., Rapoport 192 pp. $9.95 (**1993 ed.** avail. 8/92)
22 Days in China, Duke and Victor 144 pp. $7.95
2 to 22 Days in Europe, 1992 ed., Steves 276 pp. $12.95
2 to 22 Days in Florida, 1992 ed., Harris 192 pp. $9.95 (**1993 ed.** avail. 8/92)
2 to 22 Days in France, 1992 ed., Steves 192 pp. $9.95
2 to 22 Days in Germany, Austria, & Switzerland, 1992 ed., Steves 224 pp. $9.95
2 to 22 Days in Great Britain, 1992 ed., Steves 192 pp. $9.95
2 to 22 Days in Hawaii, 1992 ed., Schuchter 176 pp. $9.95 (**1993 ed.** avail. 8/92)
22 Days in India, Mathur 136 pp. $7.95
22 Days in Japan, Old 136 pp. $7.95
22 Days in Mexico, 2nd ed., Rogers and Rosa 128 pp. $7.95
2 to 22 Days in New England, 1992 ed., Wright 192 pp. $9.95
2 to 22 Days in New Zealand, 1992 ed., Schuchter 176 pp. $9.95 (**1993 ed.** avail. 8/92)
2 to 22 Days in Norway, Sweden, & Denmark, 1992 ed., Steves 192 pp. $9.95
2 to 22 Days in the Pacific Northwest, 1992 ed., Harris 192 pp. $9.95
2 to 22 Days in the Rockies, 1992 ed., Rapoport 176 pp. $9.95
2 to 22 Days in Spain & Portugal, 1992 ed., Steves 192 pp. $9.95
2 to 22 Days in Texas, 1992 ed., Harris 192 pp. $9.95 (**1993 ed.** avail. 8/92)
2 to 22 Days in Thailand, 1992 ed., Richardson 176 pp. $9.95 (**1993 ed.** avail. 8/92)
22 Days in the West Indies, Morreale and Morreale 136 pp. $7.95

Parenting Series

Being a Father: Family, Work, and Self, *Mothering* Magazine 176 pp. $12.95
Preconception: A Woman's Guide to Preparing for Pregnancy and Parenthood, Aikey-Keller 232 pp. $14.95
Schooling at Home: Parents, Kids, and Learning, *Mothering* Magazine 264 pp. $14.95
Teens: A Fresh Look, *Mothering* Magazine 240 pp. $14.95

"Kidding Around" Travel Guides for Young Readers
Written for kids eight years of age and older.

Kidding Around Atlanta, Pedersen 64 pp. $9.95
Kidding Around Boston, Byers 64 pp. $9.95
Kidding Around Chicago, Davis 64 pp. $9.95
Kidding Around the Hawaiian Islands, Lovett 64 pp. $9.95
Kidding Around London, Lovett 64 pp. $9.95
Kidding Around Los Angeles, Cash 64 pp. $9.95
Kidding Around the National Parks of the Southwest, Lovett 108 pp. $12.95
Kidding Around New York City, Lovett 64 pp. $9.95
Kidding Around Paris, Clay 64 pp. $9.95
Kidding Around Philadelphia, Clay 64 pp. $9.95
Kidding Around San Diego, Luhrs 64 pp. $9.95
Kidding Around San Francisco, Zibart 64 pp. $9.95
Kidding Around Santa Fe, York 64 pp. $9.95
Kidding Around Seattle, Steves 64 pp. $9.95
Kidding Around Spain, Biggs 108 pp. $12.95
Kidding Around Washington, D.C., Pedersen 64 pp. $9.95

"Extremely Weird" Series for Young Readers
Written for kids eight years of age and older.

Extremely Weird Bats, Lovett 48 pp. $9.95
Extremely Weird Birds, Lovett 48 pp. $9.95
Extremely Weird Endangered Species, Lovett 48 pp. $9.95
Extremely Weird Fishes, Lovett 48 pp. $9.95
Extremely Weird Frogs, Lovett 48 pp. $9.95
Extremely Weird Primates, Lovett 48 pp. $9.95
Extremely Weird Reptiles, Lovett 48 pp. $9.95
Extremely Weird Spiders, Lovett 48 pp. $9.95

Masters of Motion Series
For kids eight years and older.

How to Drive an Indy Race Car, Rubel 48 pages $9.95 paper (avail. 8/92)
How to Fly a 747, Paulson 48 pages $9.95 (avail. 9/92)
How to Fly the Space Shuttle, Shorto 48 pages $9.95 paper (avail. 10/92)

Quill Hedgehog Adventures Series
Green fiction for kids. Written for kids eight years of age and older.

Quill's Adventures in the Great Beyond. Waddington-Feather 96 pp. $5.95
Quill's Adventures in Wasteland, Waddington-Feather 132 pp. $5.95
Quill's Adventures in Grozzieland, Waddington-Feather 132 pp. $5.95

X-ray Vision Series
For kids eight years and older.

Looking Inside Cartoon Animation, Schultz 48 pages $9.95 paper (avail. 9/92)
Looking Inside Sports Aerodynamics, Schultz 48 pages $9.95 paper (avail. 9/92)
Looking Inside the Brain, Schultz 48 pages $9.95 paper

Other Young Readers Titles

The Indian Way: Learning to Communicate with Mother Earth, McLain 114 pp. $9.95
The Kids' Environment Book: What's Awry and Why, Pedersen 192 pp. $13.95
Kids Explore America's Hispanic Heritage, Westridge Young Writers Workshop 112 pp. $7.95
Rads, Ergs, and Cheeseburgers: The Kids' Guide to Energy and the Environment, Yanda 108 pp. $12.95

Automotive Titles

How to Keep Your VW Alive, 14th ed., 440 pp. $21.95
How to Keep Your Subaru Alive 480 pp. $21.95
How to Keep Your Toyota Pickup Alive 392 pp. $21.95
How to Keep Your Datsun/Nissan Alive 544 pp. $21.95
The Greaseless Guide to Car Care Confidence: Take the Terror Out of Talking to Your Mechanic, Jackson 224 pp. $14.95
Off-Road Emergency Repair & Survival, Ristow 160 pp. $9.95

Ordering Information
If you cannot find our books in your local bookstore, you can order directly from us. Please check the "Available" date above. If you send us money for a book not yet available, we will hold your money until we can ship you the book. Your books will be sent to you via UPS (for U.S. destinations). UPS will not deliver to a P.O. Box; please give us a street address. Include $3.75 for the first item ordered and $.50 for each additional item to cover shipping and handling costs. For airmail within the U.S., enclose $4.00. All foreign orders will be shipped surface rate; please enclose $3.00 for the first item and $1.00 for each additional item. Please inquire about foreign airmail rates.

Method of Payment
Your order may be paid by check, money order, or credit card. We cannot be responsible for cash sent through the mail. All payments must be made in U.S. dollars drawn on a U.S. bank. Canadian postal money orders in U.S. dollars are acceptable. For VISA, MasterCard, or American Express orders, include your card number, expiration date, and your signature, or call (800) 888-7504. Books ordered on American Express cards can be shipped only to the billing address of the cardholder. Sorry, no C.O.D.'s. Residents of sunny New Mexico, add 5.875% tax to the total.

Address all orders and inquiries to:
John Muir Publications
P.O. Box 613
Santa Fe, NM 87504
(505) 982-4078
(800) 888-7504